CATHERINE EXLEY'S DIARY

*The Life and Times
of an Army Wife
in the Peninsular War*

edited by Rebecca Probert

BRANDRAM

First published in Great Britain in 2014
by Brandram

1st edition, v. 1.0 LS

Takeaway (Publishing), 33 New Street, Kenilworth CV8 2EY

British Library Cataloguing in Publication Data.
A catalogue record for this book is available from the British Library

ISBN 978-0-9563847-9-9

Dedicated

to one of Catherine's great-great-granddaughters,

Emily Pickles-Wallis (née Woodhead)

who, in her own way, was as courageous
and resolute as Catherine, but that's another story.

Contents

INTRODUCTION

I first read Catherine's *Diary* during a rainy holiday in the Orkneys; my colleague Charlotte, knowing my interest in family history, had given me a copy to read. As soon as I began I was transfixed, realising that here was something special: the memoir of an ordinary woman who found herself in extraordinary circumstances, a personal perspective on internationally important events, a work that was simple yet vivid.

Having passed the *Diary* to other historians, it was an easy matter to persuade people to share their thoughts and areas of expertise. My Warwick University colleagues Rebecca Earle and Kirsty Hooper offered enthusiasm, insights, and suggestions for speakers, without which the project would never have got off the ground. The Faculties of Arts and Social Sciences provided funding for a symposium, enabling us to invite outside speakers: Audrey Collins from the National Archives set the *Diary* in the context of family history more generally, while Stuart Eastwood from Cumbria's Museum of Military Life spoke about the role of the 34th Regiment, in which Catherine's husband served. We were also very fortunate to have two leading experts on the role of women in the Peninsular War—Professor Charles Esdaile of the University of Liverpool, and Dr Thomas Cardoza, now of Arizona State University—as well as Warwick scholars who were able to put other aspects of Catherine's life in context.

This volume reflects the varied nature of the *Diary*. The opening chapter is written by Richard Woodhead, a descendant of Catherine, who conveys the excitement of uncovering a family tree, whether it be puzzling out the relationships between branches, sifting through original documents or—as here—discovering a voice that illuminates the bare bones of the genealogical record.

After the *Diary* itself, further chapters set it in context. Catherine's religious journey is explored by Naomi Wood, discussing the Quaker world to which Catherine's mother belonged and the Methodism that Catherine adopted later in life, and reflecting on the *Diary* as a piece of religious writing. The physical challenges of the war emerge clearly from Giorgio Riello's chapter on clothing (or its lack); so, too, does the profound importance of particular items of clothing. We have two contributions by Charles Esdaile: the first on the 34th Regiment, and a second exploring Catherine's French and Spanish counterparts, whose proximity to the theatre made them a more heterogeneous group than British army wives, and whose motivations and actions were correspondingly more varied. Thomas Cardoza compares Catherine's experiences to those of French *cantinières* (women who served as regimental 'sutlers', providing provisions), while Elodie Duché focuses on women who were, like Catherine, married to prisoners of war.

By making this important primary source more widely available we hope to assist future scholars, whether they are writing academic treatises or simply wishing to know more about how their own ancestors might have lived. Catherine's *Diary* might first have attracted interest because of the historical events she witnessed, but for many it will be the universality of her experiences of love and loss that resonate most.

Prof. Rebecca Probert, University of Warwick

DISCOVERING CATHERINE EXLEY'S STORY

By Richard Woodhead,
Catherine's great-great-great-grandson

A T JUNIOR SCHOOL, between the ages of 7 and 11 years, I very much enjoyed history. We had a very inspiring class teacher, Mr Chilton, who made the subject come alive. By the age of 8, I could recount many of the major events in the lives of most Greek mythological characters. In 1960, when I went to the Dewsbury Wheelwright Grammar School, my attitude towards history changed. I found the subject boring, dull and dusty. This was basically because the history teacher was himself boring, dull and dusty. History became to me an abstract subject to be tolerated. I dropped the subject as soon as possible and became the most left-brained engineer you would ever come across. For the next 25 years, I had no interest in history whatsoever.

So how did I become interested in Catherine Exley's story? Like most major undertakings, my investigation of my family history had very small beginnings. At the time—October 1985—our daughter Charlotte was six years old. One Sunday evening, she calmly informed us that she had to take a family tree to school the next day. As it was by now about six in the evening, some fast work had to be carried out!

My wife spoke to her mother and her late father's sister and was able to put together a basic family tree (parents, grandparents and some great grandparents). I made a telephone call to my mother in Dewsbury, West Yorkshire, who gave me the basic information about her family, but I needed details of my late father's family. During a telephone conversation with one of my aunts, she uttered the immortal words: 'You do know about Catherine Exley, do you?' She went on to tell me that Catherine had been a 'camp-follower' with Wellington's army and had accompanied her husband, a corporal. She added that Catherine was related to us, but she wasn't sure exactly how. I thought that this sounded interesting, and that I might see if I could find out a bit more.

It should be borne in mind that this was 1985—no internet, no broadband, no emails, and computers which, by today's standards, were very primitive. So genealogy was undertaken at a very slow pace, visiting churches, graveyards and libraries. The majority of research needed to take place in Yorkshire, but we lived in Worcestershire, so any activity could be done only at weekends. Occasionally, visits might be made to the centre of genealogical studies in England, the National Archives at Kew. I often describe genealogy at this time as an activity consisting of days, weeks, even months (and sometimes years) of disappointment and frustration, punctuated by brief moments of pure exhilaration. Even now in 2014, it could still be described in much the same words, though the advent of the internet—and particularly broadband—means that it is now possible to do more research in one evening than could be achieved in months in those early days.

So, where to start? I spoke again to my mother, telling her what my aunt had said. Her response was: 'Oh, Yes. Catherine was mentioned in Malcolm Haigh's book' (Malcolm being a local historian in Batley). She showed me a copy of the book, wherein was a brief reference to Catherine Exley, who in later life had run a Dame School in Batley. One of my uncles also recalled that a serialisation of some of Catherine's memoirs had been published in the local newspaper, *The Dewsbury Reporter* (issued as *The Batley News* within Batley), in the 1960s.

Today, I would have immediately searched on the internet, but not then. I used the main source of information in 1985, the local library—in this case in Batley, the town where I was born, as was Joshua Exley, Catherine's husband. There I had the pleasure of meeting Mrs Eileen Worley, one of the librarians, who could not have been more helpful. She recalled that a more complete serialisation of Catherine's memoirs had appeared in *The Dewsbury Reporter* for most of the editions covering August of 1923. Mrs Worley gave me copies of these newspapers, where I was first able to read of Catherine's exploits and privations in Spain and Portugal, where her husband was a corporal in the 34th Border Regiment, fighting the French in Wellington's army during the Peninsular War (1808-1814). Having read Catherine's memoirs, I was even more determined to find how I was related to her. I knew from my aunt that she and her brother (my father) had a grandmother, Matilda, with the maiden name Exley, so my link to Matilda at least was clear. The question was, how was Matilda related to Catherine?

Looking back at my notes from the 1980s, it is striking how slow the whole process was. From a tentative start in 1985, it was not (for example) until 1988 that I visited The National Archives (TNA) at Kew to try to look at the regimental Muster and Pay Rolls to see if I could find Joshua recruiting in Leeds, as Catherine described in her memoirs. This was a frustrating visit, with nothing found. But of course, in doing this early research, I came across other interesting information about other branches of my family tree, totally unrelated to Catherine, which slowed down progress on the Catherine front. My research was at times rather jumbled and untidy, but that is exactly how genealogical research is conducted: information is not found in a nice, orderly sequence, and instead is more like a jigsaw. The clarity of parts of the picture comes in a very random order, as does the way in which they fit together.

Initially, when making infrequent visits to Batley Library or Wakefield Archives, time seemed best spent in simply scouring the censuses and parish registers for anything which looked relevant (particularly surnames which were familiar) and then spending evenings back at home trying to fit these into what was already known. Initially, I found a Joshua Exley who appeared to be a son of Joshua and Catherine, and made the mistake of concentrating on this possibility without widening my search. Only with further research did I discover in the 1861 census a Mary Exley, widow, living in Batley with her two sons Benjamin and (yet another) Joshua and her daughter Matilda (my great grandmother), who was born around 1846. My immediate thought was that Mary must be the wife of the Joshua I had found, but this proved not to be the case. The 1841 census showed Mary, with the same two sons, married to a *Thomas* Exley, born around 1816 (regrettably, the 1841 census showed adult ages only to the nearest five years). Discovering Matilda's marriage in 1872 to one Sam Woodhead confirmed that her father was this same Thomas (who had by then died).

Much later came one of those moments of pure exhilaration. I paid yet another visit to Batley Library and looked at an original parish register. There I found an entry for the christening of a Thomas Exley, whose parents were Joshua and Catherine. Thomas was aged six years at the time. By way of explanation of this relatively old age for a christening, the vicar had added a note: 'Born in Portugal'.

Here was the link from me to my great-great-great-grand-mother Catherine and, to put the icing on the cake, I was descended from Joshua and Catherine's baby son, the only child who had survived their time in the Peninsular War!

Of course, this wasn't the end of my searching. Reading Catherine's memoirs in *The Dewsbury Reporter* had raised several questions for me. Not being an historian, especially a military one, I knew little about the Peninsular War and the lives of the combatants. For example, I had discovered Joshua and Catherine's marriage in the Leeds parish register. I knew it was the marriage of the right Joshua and Catherine, because Joshua's occupation was shown as a soldier in the 34th Regiment. Both Joshua and Catherine placed their mark against their names, which were written by the vicar who conducted the service. This suggested that neither could write. Yet clearly, Catherine could write later in life and even ran a Dame School (an early form of elementary school, before the advent of compulsory education). So when did she learn to read and write? A likely answer came, many years after I first discovered Catherine's memoirs, from a curator at the museum of the 34th Border Regiment, in Carlisle Castle.[1] He informed me that Catherine would have been taught to read and write whilst with the regiment—an early form of adult education, perhaps? Catherine, like all women 'on the strength' (i.e., as a member of the regiment) was required to work, acting as a nurse, cook or washerwoman.[2]

Another point which struck me was the need to find some corroborating evidence for Catherine's account. I had already discovered that Joshua and she were married on 19 October 1806, at St Peter's Church, Leeds, and this gave me a fixed date from which to work. Catherine related in her account that she had at one point to return to Batley as she was pregnant and so was not allowed to continue with the regiment as they set off for Madeira.[3] She said she lived in the 'poor house', which I would imagine was because she had no relations in Batley who could accommodate her, and because her parents had died some years before. If I could prove she was at the 'poor house', this would bring more certainty that Catherine's was a true account. Her memoirs show that, after they had been married for just one month, Joshua was posted with his regiment to Jersey. They were there for nine months, after which they were on the Isle of Wight for seven months. The regiment was then posted to Madeira, and Catherine returned to Batley. I came to the conclusion that Catherine would therefore have been in Batley 'poor house' around the middle of 1808 (though there could of course be some leeway in this, as journeying back and forth could add weeks to each of these events).

Visiting the Kirklees History Centre at Huddersfield Library, I asked if there were any 'registers' of residents staying in the 'poor house' in Batley about 1808. There weren't, but I was told there was a set of financial accounts. Looking through these, I read of all the expenses and the income from both the local authorities and from work done by residents to contribute to the costs of providing them with food and shelter. Imagine my delight when I discovered two entries on the 'income' side of the accounts for the month of November, 1807, both reading: 'Received from Catherine Exley for worsted spinning'. So I knew that Catherine had been back in Batley, in the poor house, in the right timescale suggested by the account of her exploits. Although this date was just 13 months after her marriage, rather than the 17 months which her memoirs suggest, it must be borne in mind that Catherine was writing her account almost fifty years after her ordeal. It is of little wonder that some of the dates might be somewhat 'hazy' after such a period of time. I also found a baptism of a child, John Exley, at All Saints' Parish Church, Batley. John was born on 5 January 1808, and baptized on 24 January, his parents being Joshua and Katherine (*sic*) Exley. It is worthy of note that John was just 19 days old at his baptism. Most infants were baptised at about 6 weeks old, so John's was swift. I concluded that Catherine was eager to get back to the regiment before it set sail: she noted in her memoirs that 'this was 3 weeks after Christmas'.

Looking at Catherine's account and George Noakes' regimental history (*A Historical Account of the Services of the 34th & 55th Regiments*, published in 1875) the 2nd Battalion of the 34th Regiment returned to Jersey in May of 1808 and remained there until mid 1809. Catherine recalled: 'This, for a soldier's life, was a very comfortable time.' On 4 June 1809, they embarked for Portugal, arriving on 4 July and (according to Catherine) disembarking two days later. Sadly, John died from a bout of measles soon after. With my wife, when on a visit to Jersey, we tried to locate the place where the regiment had stayed when posted there. We found that the barracks were not built until 1810, one year after Joshua and Catherine had been there, and concluded that they had probably camped 'under canvas'.

From The National Archives, I obtained a copy of Joshua's discharge papers, which showed that he had served in the 34th Regiment of Foot from 8 May 1805, to 2 October 1815, for 8 years and 76 days as a private, and for 2 years and 72 days as a corporal. He was then transferred to the 1st Royal Veterans Battalion, where he held the rank of corporal for a further 263 days before being discharged on 24 May 1816. More recently, I found, amongst the Napoleonic War Regimental Indexes for 1806, an entry stating that Joshua enlisted on 20 April 1805. It also stated that he had been killed on 25 July 1813. Catherine records that this day was a Sunday, when they were in the town of 'Mayhou' (her phonetic spelling of what is actually Maya, in the Pyrenees). After the Battle of Maya, when the French successfully pushed the British further back into Spain, the regiment (and Catherine) thought Joshua dead, but it turned out that he had been taken prisoner. (The Napoleonic War Regimental Indexes for 1806 also showed, immediately before Joshua's entry, the entry of his brother John, who enlisted four days after Joshua. Catherine says that he had been injured at the Battle of Vitoria. I have as yet been unable to find John's discharge papers or a definitive death date.)

The census returns for 1841 showed that by then Catherine was living in the district of Havercroft, Batley.[4] In the 1851 census, she was living in John Ward's Hill, her occupation being a bobbin winder. The Batley family historian Vivien Tomlinson[5] gave her death as 20 April 1857, a date I have more recently confirmed from the Dewsbury register of deaths.[6]

So what are my thoughts after reading and researching Catherine and Joshua's exploits? My attitude towards history has changed. When at school, history seemed to be about times long ago and far away, with little relevance to me. In a strange way, having spent a great deal of time researching my ancestor, she has now become someone very real to me. I now regard 200 years as not that long ago. I have wondered at the bravery of this lady, my great great great grandmother. Here was a woman who, in a very matter-of-fact way, wrote 'My husband… was called away [from Leeds] to Jersey. I was left behind, but followed on foot to Southampton.'[7] I struggle to find the right adjective to describe Catherine. She was brave, yes. She was determined, yes. She was compassionate, yes. She was steadfast, yes. Although I cannot find the words to adequately describe her, I can describe my feelings about her: I am proud and grateful—proud that my ancestor took part in, and survived, one of the great military campaigns of the nineteenth century; and grateful that she and her son Thomas did survive. Otherwise, I would not be here to help bring her exploits to the notice of people who might find them equally interesting.

Genealogy, of course, never stops. In my current research into Catherine's life, I am looking for her parents. There are hints in the first few sentences of her account. I know from the entry of her marriage in the Leeds parish register that her maiden name was Whitaker. Her mother, whose maiden name was Nelson, was from a wealthy Quaker family in Appleby but married a non-Quaker, which meant that she probably underwent the Quakers' 'disownment' process. Despite telephone conversations with the librarian at Friends House in London and a visit to the Family History Centre at Kendal (on the assumption that the Appleby in question was Appleby-in-Westmoreland), initial research has as yet not identified her family. I am at present researching other places called Appleby. To be successful with genealogy requires at least one of Catherine's traits. I feel that her determination never to give up has passed down through the generations to help me with my research into her remarkable life. In my research I have come to realise that not only people of high birth have interesting and important stories to tell. It is possible to find, amongst all the run-of-the-mill discoveries generated in one's research, nuggets of pure gold.

Notes

1   The museum's curators, who showed me the greatest
    kindness and patience, are Stuart Eastwood and his assistant
    Tony Goddard.

2   It has been suggested that, given the linguistic skills which
    Catherine's memoirs show, she might perhaps already have
    been able to read and write as a child; the reason she chose
    to make her mark might have been to avoid her husband
    being embarrassed that he could not sign his name.

3   Some doubt has been expressed about there being a rule in
    the regiment of not allowing pregnant women to continue
    with the battalion. It has been suggested that Catherine
    was unsuccessful in the quayside 'drawing of straws' to
    determine which women could accompany the battalion.

4   The name Havercroft has fallen into disuse as the area has
    become subsumed into central Batley. It was located in
    the area at the SE end of Commercial Street and included
    today's Hanover St., Providence St. and Hick Lane.

5   www.vivientomlinson.com

6   Batley (where Joshua was born and where both he and
    Catherine died) and Dewsbury are about 2½ miles apart.
    After 1837, Batley fell under Dewsbury Registration District.

7   A distance of about 230 miles. One cannot help but wonder
    where she stopped each night and the type of sleeping
    quarters available to her.

MAPS

Describing the events of some forty years earlier, and presumably often having known the places she passed through only from hearing their names on the lips of non-native speakers, it is no surprise that some of the places Catherine names are difficult to locate. Correct spellings (and probable locations) have been included in the text in square brackets and on the maps of the Iberian peninsula and Ireland (below).

Map 1. Southern Britain

Map 2. The Iberian Peninsula

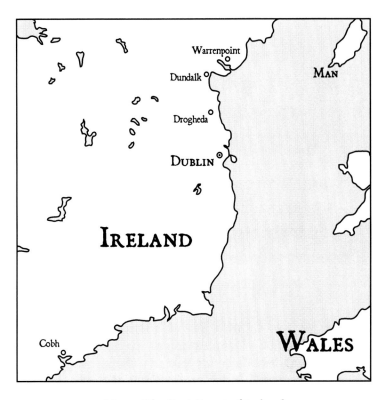

Map 3. The East Coast of Ireland

Catherine Exley's Diary

From The Dewsbury Reporter, *August, 1923*

BATLEY WOMAN'S WONDERFUL HISTORY

SOLDIER'S WIFE'S THRILLING EXPERIENCES

FOLLOWED THE ARMY IN PENINSULAR WAR

TERRIBLE PRIVATIONS IN PORTUGAL AND SPAIN

HOW SHE SAW LORD WELLINGTON

Below we give the most part of a remarkable narrative which should be of great interest to our readers. It is the story of the life of Catherine Exley, a native of Batley, who died at Havercroft, Batley, on April 20th 1857. Mrs. Exley, who was born in 1779, had a stirring and adventurous life. She followed her husband, a corporal in the 34th Regiment, right through the Peninsular War, more than 114 years ago, saw many of the battles of that historic campaign, including the battles of Salamanca and Vittoria, and suffered great privation, in the wake of the army. Her husband was taken prisoner by the French, and she returned to Batley. They settled in Batley after the war, and again suffered great hardships in the bad times that followed the war. Mrs. Exley and her family received great kindness from her neighbours in Batley. The story of her life was written by her during the twenty years preceding her death, and was printed and published in a booklet by J. W. Wood, printer, Commercial Street, Batley, in 1857. The only copy of this booklet which we have been able to discover is now in the Dewsbury Public Library, and it is through the courtesy of the librarian (Mr. W. H. Smith) that we are able to give our readers the pleasure of reading this wonderful story of the travels and adventures of a Batley woman.—EDITOR 'Reporter'.

I WAS BORN at Leeds, January 6th, 1779, and was the only child of my parents. My father was a comber in the worsted business. My mother was daughter of a wealthy Quaker at Appleby named Nelson, but her friends were so displeased with her for marrying out of their society that they never afterwards noticed her. This so preyed upon my mother's mind that her health declined, and she died of consumption. Soon after my birth my father removed to Batley, and about seven years afterwards he married again. At the age of twelve I was deprived of him also. He was a good man, and faithfully kept the promise made to my dying mother that he would be both father and mother to me. The night before his departure he affectionately pressed me to his bosom, exhorted me to do what was right, and assured me that if I did so God would raise up friends for me. These words have been strikingly verified, as all who read these pages will see. He had made his peace with God, and died happily.

I remained with my step-mother for some time after my father's death. When about 19, I engaged as servant in a family at Morley. Illness compelled me to leave this situation, and when recovered I obtained another at

Gawthorpe. It was whilst living with a family at Leeds that I first became acquainted with Joshua Exley, whom I afterwards married at the age of 26. He was one of the Militia, then recruiting at Leeds. I had no certain home, no parents, no kind friends with whom I could advise; and, alas, I knew no Heavenly Guide. Oh! how I wished for a loving mother to counsel me.

A month after our marriage, my husband, who was a corporal in the 34th Regiment under Captain Tiggers, was called away to Jersey. I was left behind, but followed on foot to Southampton. We embarked there for Jersey, and had a most perilous voyage, being twice driven through the Needles. We lay at Jersey nine months, and afterwards at the Isle of Wight seven months, whence we were ordered to Madeira, and such women as had families were prohibited from accompanying their husbands. I was near the period of confinement, and was therefore obliged to return to Batley; the overseers there kindly recommended me to the poor-house, which in my case was only such in name, for every comfort was afforded me.

In the meantime, my husband and his comrades were delayed by contrary winds, and put back to Ireland. As the fleet had sailed, I received a letter from him, with the intimation that he would shortly be in England. He arrived at Stenning, near Chichester, where I joined him. Through the kind contributions of my neighbours I did not set out penniless, and was enabled to travel by waggon from Leeds for the sum of 15s., after which I met with an innkeeper who had formerly lived at Leeds, and who, recognising me as an old neighbour, sent me in a return chaise to within twelve miles from him I anticipated meeting.

I had now only one remaining sixpence, with which I sent my small wardrobe by coach, having my infant to carry. My husband, on hearing I was so near, got two of his comrades who were on furlough to come and meet me, as he could not leave until after evening parade. Calling at an inn to warm my baby, a kindly gentleman gave me a shilling, and ordered me some refreshment. I was accompanied by a woman from B------, also going to join her husband. At eight in the evening we were still eight miles from the barracks, and after many fruitless inquiries for those who we knew were on the look-out, we determined to remain all night on the way. A bed of straw was prepared, but ere we had composed ourselves to sleep, we were gladdened by the arrival of our husbands, with whom we returned.

This was three weeks after Christmas. Seven days after we marched to Chichester; thence, after a lapse of three months, we embarked a second time, at Portsmouth, for Jersey, where we lay ten months. This, for a soldier's life, was a very comfortable time, though we were rather at a loss for fire. The widow of a sea captain residing here wished me to share her loneliness, but I preferred accompanying my husband to Portugal. For leave to do so, our colonel wrote to the general, and, having obtained consent, we embarked June 4th. After a pleasant passage (excepting the usual accompaniment of a first voyage, sea-sickness), we disembarked July 6th, and encamped at Alcantor [Alcântara], in the suburbs of Lisbon. Here our boy, to our very great sorrow, took the measles, sickened, and died.

Three weeks after, the recruiting parties joined, and the women belonging to the Army were left for safety in the camp. My child lived only six weeks after his father left me in the camp. I was at this time penniless, and without a bed save the naked earth on which to lay. All our baggage had been ordered to be sent on board, reserving only a change of linen; these articles were never recovered, for the vessel returned to England, and after so long a time the expense attending their restoration would have exceeded their value.

Our accommodations at this time were very wretched; damp walls, and the floors not boarded. I sewed some garments together and stuffed them with straw, on which I deposited my poor boy. The captain, advancing me money on account of my husband, enabled me to procure a coffin, reserving half-a-crown for the clergyman. My boy was buried October 14th, after the English mode of interment, which last sad office being performed according to the custom of my native land afforded me much satisfaction.

My little girl was born about this time, and I should have been in a most destitute condition but that the day before I went into the officers' room to ask permission to boil a little water, when my voice was recognised by the corporal, who, with a regiment of Dragoons, had formerly been quartered at the Cooper's Arms, Wakefield, where I lived in the capacity of servant. They gave up their room to me, and thus was my condition greatly improved. They liberally provided me with tea, chocolate, butter, etc., ordered my woman to take the kettle daily to the mess-room for soup, and paid her wages; lent me their blankets and cloaks, and in many other ways kindly assisted me. I had written several letters to my husband, in one of which I sent a lock of hair belonging to the dear little deceased, but was prevented receiving any intelligence lest communications should reach the Spaniards from the French. Having had no tidings for a long time, I became very anxious, and, with the colonel's leave, I walked barefoot to Lisbon, a distance of three leagues, and whence I returned by boat. It appeared, however, that the regiment had no settled quarters, and the attempt to find my husband was unsuccessful. Here I had a most dangerous attack of dysentery, which greatly enfeebled me. My baby also endured great sufferings, and was reduced to a mere shadow.

About this time, I was the painful witness of a dreadful scene of horror occasioned by a cruel Portuguese, who cut open an Englishman. To such deadly violence were they thereby provoked that an earthquake which happened at the time was not perceived.

It was usual for a sentry to be posted so that he could overlook the rooms, and on one occasion he heard my moan, and, not knowing whence it came, was frightened off his post through supernatural fears. Corporal Beer inquired into the cause, and found me lying on the floor, with my infant in my arms. His wife made a charcoal fire; coffee and other nourishments at length revived me. Here I was attended night and day until I could move about.

A party of the 16th Regiment now came from Abrantes, and their quarter-master offered to pay my expenses in rejoining my husband, of whom I had by this time heard. In seven days I was with him, and the next day they stormed a castle [at Campo Maior].

A fever at this time ravaging the troops, my husband was directed to attend the sick to Lisbon, but ere long the contagion seized him and he was carried to the general hospital. I did not long escape and was taken to the house set apart for the women. For some time we were both too ill and insensible to care much for each other's welfare, but when able he rejoined his Regiment at Salamanca. After much hardship and difficult marching, he was sent with more sick to Abrantes, which was an easier but not more pleasant duty than following the colonel. He again caught the fever, and was returned to the hospital. A short time before, I had buried my little girl. This was on the 12th October. On the 14th the sick were put on board.

On the recovery of his health, I and my husband were sent on shore to join the regiment at Apellon, in Spain [probably Alpalhão, in Portugal]. Here much fatigue had to be encountered—after advancing by day to retreat at night. On one occasion the French had gone on a plundering expedition to Boroughoe [probably Arroyomolinos] and the English went to intercept the party.

The colonel now procured my husband the office of ward master, whilst I nursed the sick and took care of the provisions.

About this time, the battle of Albuera was fought. The women were left in charge of the baggage until the ground of encampment was ploughed with cannon shot. Trees were cut down to bury the corpses. We encamped all night in a wood. After the action there was a terrible storm of thunder and lightning, so that all appeared in a blaze.

At Elva [i.e., Elvas] great preparations were made to receive Lord Wellington. The windows were decked with flowers, rosemary, etc., and the occasion of his entry was hailed with triumph.

At this time my third child was born. My life was despaired of on account of extreme weakness and I lost the use of my left side for a time.

Just then the French were strong against us. The sick were removed in cars drawn by bullocks. A nurse accompanied our party, and we were provided with a comfortable house and warm hearth within a mile of the French. At 16 days old, my infant was brought to me a corpse, having died of convulsions. My husband had been reduced to such a state of weakness by repeated sickness that for six weeks he was kept ignorant of this bereavement. In two months, all efficient men were ordered to join their regiments. We remained three months at a small village in Spain, the enemy retreating and allowing us to rest before we came to Salamanca.

While laying at a village near Arinjos [Aranjuez] the adjutant's wife was attacked with fever, and as I had the advantage of experience, having been nurse for some time at a hospital, the adjutant wished me to attend upon his wife during her indisposition.

I obtained leave to do so, but at the end of a fortnight was seized with the same malady myself. My hair was cut off, and while still in a state of great weakness and delirium we were ordered to Arinjos. I was placed upon a mule, on which my husband with a little assistance supported me.

On the fourth day after our arrival the French entered the town about four in the afternoon. Immediately, the English army was ordered to cross the bridge, and when the whole body had passed over we set fire to it to prevent the enemy overtaking us. We encamped in a wood. I was still very ill, and, having no medical assistance, no comfortable provisions, nothing but the cold ground on which to repose my feeble limbs, my prospects of speedy recovery were not very cheering. But the Lord strengthened me, even under such discouraging circumstances; nothing is too hard or difficult for His Almighty arm to accomplish.

The following day the sick were ordered to Lisbon, and it unfortunately happened that on their way thither they were all taken prisoners by the French. I was unwilling to leave the Regiment, and having providentially taken refuge in a private house which contained a few invalids I escaped this disaster.

After a few days I was conveyed in the commissary's car to the outskirts of Madrid, where our regiment was then encamped. Two hours after our arrival we were again compelled to fly for safety from the enemy. We made for a wood, wading through a river the water of which reached as high as our waists. In this miserably wet state, and on a cold, frosty night, I slept on the hard ground with my infant boy in my arms. I cannot express what my feelings were during this long, weary night. My bodily weakness returned. I arose, shivering with cold, and as the enemy was between us and our provisions, I had no comfortable refreshment.

The regiment was formed for battle, and prepared for an engagement. During my residence in Portugal, I derived considerable advantage from possessing a knowledge of the language. On this occasion I went to an adjoining village, and, being able to make known my wants, I obtained a little wine and bread, which I took to share with my husband, and on my return brought away his watch. I knew not then that I should ever see him alive again, but the Lord mercifully preserved him. The French retreated, and we advanced about three leagues further into the country before we encamped for the night.

We marched onward a few leagues every day until we reached Salamanca, and encamped on the plains. Here we were suddenly surprised by the report of the enemy's near approach. I well remember that day; it was that on which I saw for the first time in my life the then Lord Wellington. I was seated on a hill-side, giving nourishment to my infant, when I heard him say to Generals Hill and Stewart, 'We must return to the hill with all speed, or the French will take possession of it.' My husband volunteered his services (for other duties had been allotted to him that day), always foremost to face danger. By great dispatch the summit was attained before the enemy arrived.

After an engagement of two hours, our regiment fell back and encamped for the night. We received no refreshment but a pint of wheat to each person. The same evening the women were ordered to join the baggage waggons. At Salamanca we met with a Spaniard who had seven loaves to dispose of; they each weighed about three pounds, for which we paid five shillings. We made the purchase with eager delight and the loaves were divided. We longed to rejoin the regiment but were at a loss to find it or what route to take. After some consideration, I observed to my companion that I would go in which path soever the Lord directed me (but not with the feeling which would now dictate such a determination). I set out, and they all followed me. We had not walked more than half a mile before we met with the regiment. I carried my half loaf under my arm, and it was immediately perceived. The men anxiously enquired from whence it came, and whether more was to be bought. The officer tried to induce me to part with it by offering a large sum of money, but gold was of no use in our present circumstances. He and some others were so urgent upon me that I could not refrain from cutting off a few slices, and thus parting with some of the food I had intended for my poor husband, who had marched a long way under a heavy burden, and had found no subsistence save a few acorns. Being a corporal, he was serving out, when I first perceived him, a small quantity of rum to the men.

We had three leagues further to advance, but I was so weary that I feared to undertake the journey. However, a sargeant kindly offered to carry my child for me on his knapsack, and I followed. The rain poured down the whole way, and the road was so bad that we walked above the knees in mire and wet. The sand got amongst my clothes, which, rubbing against my body, caused acute pain in walking. In this state, we encamped for the night.

The rain still came down in torrents, so that it was with the greatest difficulty any fire could be kept burning, the fuel was so wet. After many fruitless attempts, a cradle was sacrificed by one of the women, and with it a little fire was made. Some bran was found in a neighbouring mill, with which a sort of porridge was made; but I could not eat any of it. Some boughs were cut down from the trees, and on these I reposed my weary limbs. Having neither tents nor beds, everyone was provided with a blanket only; the one which covered me was soaked with water.

We were to march at four. I rose so stiff and cold that I could scarcely put a foot to the ground. We halted after a march of two leagues, and soon after were surprised by the near approach of the enemy. When the alarm was given I was putting on a pair of regimental shoes belonging to my husband, having previously thrown aside a pair of worn-out boots, which had never been taken off since the first day of wearing, about three months before. I snatched up my boy, and, leaving everything else behind me, we crossed a river (which was very deep) three abreast. One woman who remained behind to pack up her property lost her life for refusing to surrender it to the enemy.

We spent the night in a wood, and the next morning we were ordered to Therigo [probably Ciudad Rodrigo], which was five leagues distant. I was harrassed both in mind and body, for we had got separated from the regiment. I was thankful of the opportunity of exchanging a gill of rum for a few biscuits with a German soldier, which I prepared for my boy. The women had my legs to rub for some time before I could stand, and then I had to carry my boy 15 miles. Having started first, I lost my way, and not meeting with anyone who could direct me I wandered on till four in the afternoon, when I encountered part of the 7th Division, who were chiefly Germans. With them I crossed a river, taking hold of a horse's bridle with one hand to prevent my sinking, and holding my boy above the water with the other. We found the remainder of the division encamped in a wood. I had scarce reached them before the enemy surrounded the baggage at the very place whence we had but that moment escaped. I stood trembling by a small fire, when a young man belonging to our company, who had also lost his way, came up. The meeting was delightful to both. He invited me to eat of a lamb which he had found. I did so with great relish, though the flesh was scarcely warmed through.

An officer now came and ordered us two leagues further. It was a dismal night; the rain came down in torrents, and the roads were miserably bad. After having walked about four miles, I became too weary to proceed, and, perceiving a party who had encamped by the road side, I asked permission to warm myself and child at a small fire which they had lighted. I laid the dear babe on one of the saddles, enveloped in my [*unclear*—'cloak'?]. Some beef was boiling on the fire, but the men had neither salt nor bread. The water in which it had boiled was given to me. After reposing about two hours, I was aroused by another alarm of the enemy's approach, and we were quickly ordered to proceed. I rose in great terror, but for some time was unable to stand, and it was only by hard rubbing that I recovered the use of my limbs. Taking my boy on my back, I hastened onwards. I had not proceeded far when a waggon with one of the large guns, driven at full speed, came in contact with me, and I received a violent shock, which forced me into a deep ditch, where I lay to all appearance dead. However, I was conveyed to an old building which had formerly been a convent, and the next morning, proper restoratives having been applied, on recovering my senses, I found myself by a large fire made with sticks, and several women attending me.

The following day I hoped to accomplish the remaining two leagues to Hollingo [possibly Santa Olalla de Yeltes], but the state of the roads compelled me once more to stay and sleep, and to such a desponding state was I brought that I almost hoped I might never rise again. Yes, in my blind ignorance I wished to die, but that desire was mercifully forbidden; yet I had no prospect of being removed from my uncomfortable resting-place unless for burial. For 28 days a few biscuits were my only nourishment; my clothes were covered with filth and vermin from having been six weeks without a change of linen.

At last I ventured to start, but had not proceeded far before I was utterly exhausted. With my child clasped in my arms, I lay under a hedge for about an hour, when we were discovered by a sergeant who had charge of a car drawn by bullocks, into which he was gathering the sick, and the knapsacks of those who had died. An officer who accompanied him offered me some brown bread out of his haversack, but I was quite unable to eat. He took the child, and had me lifted into the car, whence we proceeded to Radeugo [Ciudad Rodrigo].

How powerfully are my feelings awakened by the recollection of this interposition! Had not the Lord softened the hearts of those around me, inclining them to deal thus gently with me, I could not have lived to return to my native country, but in my case, while many lay neglected by the wayside gasping for breath, I was specially provided for; an Almighty arm was extended for my deliverance, though I felt it not.

Whilst on the road I was attacked with a violent ague, and had to be left in a comfortless empty building with damp floors. The sergeant procured me a blanket, and I used the best means in my power for my recovery. In about four days I was able to stir about a little, when, to my unspeakable joy, I received intelligence of my husband's regiment, which was halting at a neighbouring town. The colonel, hearing of my situation, was so considerate as to send my husband here on duty in charge of the sick for the hospitals that he might have an opportunity of looking out for me. After many fruitless searches and diligent inquiries, he began to despair of receiving further tidings of me; however, after two days, orders were given for the men and women to parole, that they might be dismissed to join their respective regiments. As I was proceeding out of town, one of the 34th on sentry at the gates exclaimed: 'Oh! Mrs. Exley; the corporal is almost broken-hearted about you, he is on duty at the other end of the town.' I need not dwell on our feelings of joy and delight at meeting together after such a period of fearful suspense and extreme suffering. His appearance was truly deplorable. I found him in the guard room, with his clothes in a most ragged state, and comfortless in the extreme.

Next morning we were put into an old house without roof, and after parading were dismissed to our regiment, which we joined the following day. In crossing a very deep river, one of our company was drowned, but fortunately for us, just as we got to the river's brink, one of the 10th was crossing on horseback and took our boy along with him, and returned twice for my husband and me.

I oft lament that I could all this time be so blind as not to recognise the hand of a protecting Providence under all these wonderful preservations. How much time have I thus irretrievably lost, and how little remains in which to praise Him!

We met our regiment with feelings of mingled joy, each congratulated his comrade on his safety, and all deplored the lost. For my first provisions I paid half-a-crown for a pound of flour and one shilling for a pound of salt, which I procured through the medium of the sergeant-major; and thus I was once more able to make some bread, though without yeast, of which we partook very sparingly to some chocolate. But not withstanding these restrictions, so long had been our fast, that the effects of our eating were such as to cause both of us to be apprehensive of death. Our legs and bodies swelled considerably, and many of the men were obliged to exercise their limbs with cricket and football. After being in quarters five days, I was painful to find that we had not more than twenty men on parade, so sad were the effects of the fatiguing marches which our division underwent.

On Christmas Day we arrived at Catelas [most likely Casas de Don Gómez, but possibly Cadalso, in the Sierra de Gata]. A small remainder we were. Some had been taken prisoners, and others were wandering they knew not wither. Here we had an opportunity of purchasing every necessary, providing fresh clothing, and making ourselves tolerably comfortable. The enemy, too, fatigued and out of reach of provisions, willingly allowed themselves a rest of four months. When spring arrived, having recruited our strength and stragglers having joined the force, we began to advance. The first time we met with the enemy was at Vittoria [*sic*]. The evening before the action, Bonaparte had boasted in a ballroom how easily he should defeat the English on the morrow. On this same night we were encamped on a hillside, and at two in the morning we were ordered to march, though little expecting to engage that day. As we passed along, the fires on the road showed where the French had encamped the night before. After marching in double quick time, the colonel called a halt, and ordered the men to load their guns and fix their bayonets. As usual, I marched with the regiment. As I was loosing down my husband's ammunition, thc coloncl, in passing by, askcd me to remain with the men all day. I found a quantity of rice that had been left by the enemy, and though I had often heard they were in the habit of putting poison in the food thus left behind them, I could not resist the temptation of eating, and allowing my child to partake of the rice also, for I felt that if we refrained we might die of hunger, not being able to get at our provisions. I know not how to describe the scenes I witnessed on this awful day. The first shock given to my feelings arose from the sight of a man's head severed from the body and sent a considerable distance by a gun. He had been met by a skirmishing party (or picquet) who had thus deprived him of life. This was about a mile from the field of battle, and as I walked along I saw the road covered with blood which had streamed from the wounds of the men, who were continually being carried to the rear, previous to being removed to the general hospital.

The climate is dreadfully hot, and numbers died for want of care. I advanced to the plains and offered my assistance to the surgeons. They were very busily employed. It is impossible for me to describe the agony of the poor creatures as they lay weltering in their blood and gasping for breath. I tore the linen off my back to bind up their wounds and was instantly employed fetching water to quench the thirst of the dying. Many perished for lack of proper medical care and attention. I began to be very anxious about my dear husband, whose body I feared every moment to find amongst the slain. I was turning over first one and then another till dusk, when a drummer approached and assured me my husband was living safely somewhere. He had come to seek a knapsack, as his own had been taken away when he was engaged in the conveyance of the wounded. After dark, he accompanied me and some other women to a village near, and, finding an empty house, we lay down on the floor to sleep, all ignorant of the fate of our husbands. The drummer offered us food, but we felt more desirous of rest, and therefore declined it till next morning. At daybreak we went towards the town in search of the regiment, when we saw a number of French prisoners laid under sheds, some maimed and others severely wounded, some without arms and others without legs, some deprived of one limb and some of another. Our army had taken the wife of Bonaparte in her carriage, who was exchanged next day for some of our officers who had been taken.

We stripped the French of everything they had—baggage, ammunition, boots, money, etc. Many enriched themselves by plundering the dead, but I did not take a single crown, for I had other objects of greater interest to engage my attention.

Having received intelligence at Vittoria, we proceeded onwards, and found our army encamped about three leagues from the town. They had no bread, but were serving out a little rum. The sight of me filled my husband's eyes with tears; he seized my hand, and for several minutes we were unable to speak. When his feelings had partly subsided, he said: 'Catherine, the Lord has spared us to me again.' He looked dreadfully ill from the exertions of the previous day. Sixty rounds of ammunitions were discharged at the first onset; and when more arrived they formed into line again. The barrel of my husband's gun was so hot that he was obliged to hold it with the cuff of his coat. The men's faces were completely blackened with the smoke and the powder.

We had now to advance three leagues further. I was so weak from yesterday's fatigue (for during most of the time I was so painfully and laboriously employed I carried my child on my back) that I told my husband I really could not walk any further. He encouraged me to try, and got the child placed on an ass. It was nearly ten at night when we reached our resting place, and during the night our outlying picquets were engaged with the enemy. Next morning we began our march to Myhou [Maya], the highest part of the Pyrenees. Alas! it was there my poor husband was taken prisoner. In going down the hills, which were very steep and slippery, we were exposed to great danger, and were compelled to take off our shoes and walk barefoot. The ascent was still more arduous. I had to crawl up on my hands and feet, having my child on my back. On our march we had to pass through an immense forest, the largest I ever saw. The road was excellent, but there was not a single house to be seen for many days.

We were some weeks in reaching the heights, but when the task was achieved we rested a fortnight. On the Sunday we attended Divine service. According to custom, a level plain was chosen, and the troops formed a circle. The minister stood in the centre, with his book placed on a big drum. We had but just assembled when our sentinels gave an alarm, and the men immediately advanced to the mountains. When the French saw our position they retreated. The following Sunday they did the very same thing. Had they not mistaken our small party for a picquet, and supposed the main body to be at hand, they would not have retreated, and we must inevitably have fallen into their hands.

The following week we removed towards the town of Myhou, and our position was taken up by another detachment. We lay here about ten days, when we were again disturbed, and this time also on a Sunday, 25th July. About ten o'clock a sergeant had brought us an account of the recovery of my husband's brother, who was in the same regiment and had been wounded at Vittoria. We were just writing to his mother some account of these proceedings, not having the slightest idea of an attack. My husband had a mark on one of his fingers, which had been wounded some years before when cutting some grass, and I had observed that if any mischance happened him I should be able to recognise him from this mark. The words had scarce been uttered before General Hill's aide-de-camp came galloping up, with orders instantly to strike the tents, and every man to be ready to fall in at a moment's warning, and not to leave the camp ground. Our rations were served out, and the men ordered to prepare dinner at once. They got their kettles to fetch the water in which to boil the meat, when the word was given to 'fall in' immediately. They threw down their kettles, and in a few minutes not a single man was to be seen. To our surprise, on looking towards the hill, we perceived the enemy had got possession of it. It seems three of our German soldiers had deserted and informed the enemy of our real strength. It was a sad disaster! Our colonel was brought back with his leg shot off, and the men had suffered a great loss in attempting to recover the hill. They had no chance against the more numerous enemy. I longed to see my husband return, if even wounded, but this was not to be my lot. We retreated from the camp, and arrived at Pampeluna [Pamplona] the next day. When night came on, I laid my head on a stone for a pillow, and fell into a kind of dose, when I was aroused by the tramp of feet, caused by the approach of the regiment. I enquired anxiously about Exley. One of the men incautiously said, 'He is shot dead,' at which I dropped down insensible under an officer's horse, who kindly alighted and gave me some cordial, which restored me to consciousness. There were only a few of our men remaining, and one of them informed me of the particulars of my husband's death, and where it took place. I had no doubt of the truth of the statement, and thought if I could but reach the spot and cover his poor body with the earth I should be thankful.

We halted on the other side of the town, and although I made diligent enquiry I could not for some time gain further intelligence of the object of my search, and when I did the same sad news was repeated. Our troops continued to retire, and were harrassed continually, being surrounded on all sides, so that we scarce knew which way to turn for fear of the enemy. On the ninth day we arrived at the place where we had encamped previous to the engagement. I obtained leave for two men to accompany me to bury my husband, in the mournful hope of being able to recognise his remains, but an Almighty arm had protected his body, reserving his soul for eternal glory. When we arrived at the field the dead were so discoloured as scarcely to look as if they were English troops, being turned quite black.

After turning over several of the bodies we found that of a corporal in the very place where it had been said my husband met his death. On examining his clothing I thought I knew it, and cried out, 'He is here,' but there was no appearance of the mark on his finger; otherwise, I should have been convinced of his identity. We were employed in this mournful duty three days—women in search of their husbands, officers in search of their brother officers. During this time, so much was I absorbed in trouble that I was scarcely sensible of the noxious effluvia, but which was so seriously felt by the men that they were obliged to leave me to my task. The colonel and officers were quite lavish in their kindness, allowed me my husband's rations extra, appointed me to sleep with a sargeant's wife, and assured me of redress if I met with any incivility. All my necessities were supplied, and I was advised to stay with the regiment till I could with safety return to England.

On the 29th of January, two ladies from the 39th which belonged to our brigade, though not to our regiment—for there are three regiments in a brigade—sent myself and child a present of some linen. I had occasionally washed for them, and was told to go every three days to their marquees or tent for whatever I required. To the best of my recollection, I remained about three months with the regiment where it then lay. We suffered many hardships from the inclement state of the weather. The luxury of dry clothing was very seldom known. I usually sat (for it would have been almost certain death to lie down) with my boy on my knee, the waters pouring down from the sky and mountain with extreme rapidity and without cessation. We afterwards removed to within a short distance of the place where I was told my husband had been killed. I rejoiced at this opportunity of having another search. It was after dark when we arrived; the place being on the line of march between Spain and France, the men were ordered to cut down trees, of which to make batteries to intercept the enemy. Daylight discovered that our tents had been pitched on a field of battle, and the number of slain around marked it out as the place where Lord Wellington had been engaged some time before.

The colonel ordered some of the men on fatigue duty to inter the bodies, but so putrid had they become that it was dangerous to disturb them, so they covered them slightly with earth as they lay. We suffered severely from scarcity of water for some time. So variable, however, is the climate that a most terrific storm of thunder, lightning, and rain was experienced here. The firelocks attracted the lightning so much that there seemed one continuous blaze of light until the men covered them with their coats. In the morning we found that all the bodies which had so lately been covered were washed bare again, and this caused such a horrid stench that a pestilence was apprehended. The doctors ordered a small quantity of brandy to each man, and immediate removal from the spot. We accordingly marched to the heights of Myhou [Maya], on the Pyrenees. We ascended the mountain with difficulty and encamped, exchanging positions with another regiment every three days. When on the lofty heights of the mountain we lay so near the clouds and there was such a constant drizzle and rain that we were often unable to distinguish each other.

On the ninth day we marched back to Roncosvalles [*sic*], where we were to remain until we received a fresh supply of clothing. The colonel presented me with £1, and the officers generally contributed two dollars each, some more, but none less, so that with what was due to me for washing and these kind presents I received amounted together to twelve guineas. I had a very creditable recommendation for my journey to satisfy the public in case of any accident that I was no impostor. My complexion, height, and age were given, as also those of my child. With such a passport, I could command 1 1/2 d. a mile for myself and 1 d. for my child. It was signed by the general, and I was to call on the agent, Mr. McDonald, Pall Mall Court, London, who was treasurer of the fund, the regiment being out of cash. Besides, if I had been possessed of more property, they feared I might be stripped of it by the treacherous Spaniards. I gave my money to the quartermaster, who was to see me on board. Just as I was leaving the camp and seating myself on the mule which was to convey me, the two ladies before named came up, shook hands with me, and gave me two dollars each, as also some change. I had some time before bought a coarse cloth sheet of one of the inhabitants, with the intention of reserving it for my husband's corpse, but which I now converted into articles of dress.

After a toilsome journey, we at length reached the place of embarkation. The quartermaster went to the agents of the transports about to sail for dear old England, and secured me a passage in one free of expense. Having received my money from him, I purchased some tea, sugar, and other articles for the voyage. As I was so subject to sea sickness, I was grieved to find that I was the only woman going on board this vessel, but just as I was bidding adieu to my kind friends I was accosted by an Englishwoman from Colchester; she, too, was going out in another vessel alone. After reasoning together, I proposed that she should apply to the agent for permission to go together. To this she seemed reluctant, but on my offering to accompany her we went together to him. I showed my testimonials, and our request to sail together was very willingly granted. He [unclear] great sympathy and interest in my trials, and gave me a recommendation to the captain of the transport, who received me in the kindest manner, and requested me to ask freely for everything I required. He frequently took my child on his lap, and fed it with the choicest morsels. There were also on board three French officers (prisoners) and two English officers going to Stilton. As we were leaving the harbour a violent storm arose, which caused the total wreck of one vessel and the loss of most of the crew. After being in danger of a similar fate, our vessel managed to regain the harbour.

Next morning we sailed again, but met with such rough weather in the Bay of Biscay that we were driven back into harbour. Another attempt was made, but the wind was still contrary. More than once we were driven near the French coast, where we might easily have fallen into their hands. On these stormy waves we were tossed about three weeks before we reached Falmouth, which we ought to have accomplished in about a week had the weather been favourable.

We had intended anchoring at Plymouth, but were prevented. I and my companion had suffered so much that the captain gave us leave to go on shore before the Custom House officers had examined the vessel. At Falmouth we met with a very kind friend, a widow, who kept a small canteen or public-house. She opened her house for our reception, and assisted me to purchase mourning for myself and boy, and, besides this, she and her daughter sat up all night to sew for me. Thus in every strait and difficulty the Lord made a way for me. My companion met with a severe disappointment; she, like myself, was compelled to throw her old clothes overboard, but was not so fortunate in obtaining new apparel. It had been obtained at St. Sebastian, when leave was given to plunder the city for the treachery of the inhabitants, who poured boiling water on our troops after they had freely opened their gates for our reception, upon which Lord Wellington caused the city to be plundered and burnt.

My companion on the voyage and I were very reluctant to part, as we resolved to travel together to London, to which place I paid her fare in the waggon. We should have had a comfortable journey had I been well, but I was far from being so; besides that, the nearer I approached my native country the more harrassed were my feelings and the more I deplored the loss which I imagined I had sustained. The landlady at whose house I slept in town advised me to have a guide to conduct me to the agent, who resided at Pall Mall. From him I expected to receive three guineas out of the regimental fund, but as the colonel had been prevented by other engagements from writing to him he could not give me my money. He, however, gave me a paper which I was to take to Lodge coffee-house. It was an order for £25, to which all widows are entitled, whose husbands have been slain on the field of battle. Here, again, I had a paper put into my hands, and was informed that it must be signed by the clergy and magistrates of my own parish before I could obtain possession of this sum of money.

It was on the 5th November 1814 that I took my fare for myself and boy on the waggon bound for Leeds. We travelled night and day, and the weather was very stormy. To me it felt very cold and searching, after having lived so long in a hot climate. We arrived at Leeds on the 12th. I forwarded my luggage to Batley, part of which consisted of three blankets, of which I was very glad, as I knew I should have no home to go to, nor perhaps even a bed to lie on. I had a brother in Leeds, at whose house I remained all night. The following morning I accidentally met with one of my old neighbours, who accosted me by name, and informed me that a letter waited for me at his mother's from Exley. I was greatly agitated by this intelligence, and could not believe what I heard. I exclaimed 'Oh that I too was in France, and a prisoner!' for such, as I was informed, was my poor husband's lot. I blamed myself much for not having made minute enquiries before I came to England.

Of all my wearisome journeys, I think none ever appeared more tedious than this from Leeds, I was so anxious and impatient to peruse my letter. Many of my friends and neighbours came to meet me, and one kindly offered me a horse to ride on; but no-one had the forethought to bring the letter, and that was what I was most anxious to see. As I drew near the village, the people left their houses and came out in crowds, to meet me; but I could not speak a word. The letter was read to me several times before I could understand its contents, or feel assured that it really was written by my husband. He told me that he was a prisoner of war in Gurt prison [i.e., Guéret, in France]; that he was tolerably comfortable, and was glad to hear that I and the child were returned to England.

I spent a fortnight in visiting my friends and neighbours, who when at leisure were glad to hear a relation of my adventures. The kindness and exceeding generosity of one in particular, I never can forget. Though quite a stranger to me, he received me and my child into his house, discharged a debt which I owed, and he and his kind wife treated us both as members of their family. I replied to my husband's letter, and also wrote to the colonel, who had not then received the returns from France, and was therefore ignorant of my husband's situation. Of course I did not apply for the £25; but the clergyman of the district very kindly undertook to procure for me the three guineas due to me out of the fund money.

My husband was a prisoner nine months. Before being released, he and the other prisoners were marched about the country from one place to another, lest they should be discovered and rescued by the allies. At this time he received a shock to his constitution from which he never quite recovered, and which ultimately obtained for him his discharge. When peace was proclaimed, he was released from prison, and sent to Bordeaux, where he was sumptuously entertained in a kind gentleman's family. He was accommodated with a feather bed, and the best of everything the house afforded. How great the change, after undergoing excessive fatigue and the privations of a prison! After spending a week there, he embarked with the regiment in a vessel for Ireland.

It had been reported that the Irish were about to rebel again, and therefore it was deemed expedient to send a strong body of troops. As soon as I received intelligence from Ireland, I set out on my journey thither; from Leeds to Manchester, and thence to Liverpool, I travelled by coach. I was detained here by contrary winds for nearly a fortnight. There was such a hurricane, that it blew the slates off the houses, and made it dangerous to walk along the streets.

I paid my fare to Dublin, and met with several of our soldiers, who had been on furlough, and were going over in the same vessel. To our dismay we discovered that the captain and most of his men were intoxicated; and the vessel was several times in danger of being lost. We were in great alarm for four days, fearing that we should be driven on the rocks; but at length we arrived safely in harbour, off Waring's Point [Warrenpoint], Newry. My slender wardrobe was completely spoilt by the salt water. It was Christmas Day when we landed, and I had only a trifling sum left. I was still nearly one hundred miles from my husband, tho' had all been favourable we ought to have landed within a mile of Dublin. My little boy wore a pair of stockings which my kind friend the widow had knitted for me, and these I gave for my first night's lodgings. Unfortunately, I allowed the sergeant, who was proceeding to Dublin by coach, to take my clothes along with him, some of which I ought to have retained by me to pay my way. My bed was nothing but a heap of straw: I proceeded next morning with my clothes still wet on my back, having had no opportunity of drying them in my cold comfortless lodgings.

Before evening we arrived at D----- [presumably Dundalk] a distance of eighteen miles, having had only a scanty meal of potatoes, which had been given us on the road. Some of our soldiers lay here, and one of the officers billetted us. We then reached Droekedy [Drogheda], but here I became too ill to proceed, and my fellow-travellers were compelled to leave me, in a hut as miserable as any Irish cabin could possibly be. I requested them to ask leave for my husband to come to me, or that some money might be sent to me. It appeared, however, that he was ill in the hospital, and I was three days and nights dependent on casual relief. Poor as my accommodations were, sixpence a night was demanded for them; but I had no money wherewith to discharge the sum owing.

On the fourth morning a soldier who had formerly lived in Leeds, entered the hut, and seeing me, enquired if I was one of the party which had been shipwrecked? On hearing my case, he urged me to accompany him to the barracks, where I should meet some of my countrywomen, who would be rejoiced to receive me. I however refused to leave, on account of the sum I owed for my lodgings. Soon after, he sent a loaf of bread for our breakfast and speedily came back with the sum required: we both accompanied him to the barracks, where we were received with great cordiality, the women provided us with a change of linen, washed our clothes, and made us once more comfortable. In the short space of a week, I wrote three letters to Dublin, but without receiving any reply: this was a great trouble to me; But about the ninth day a man came from the hospital where my husband lay. He was attended by a corporal's guard, for protection against the insurgents. I asked the corporal respecting the 34th, and he informed me that part of the regiment still lay at Dublin, but that some had gone to the Indies. I now thought of my unanswered letters, and feared that Exley was of the latter party.

However, after further conversation, I learned his situation, and that he was in great trouble on account of a report in a newspaper that the vessel in which I had sailed was lost. It originated in the obstinacy of the man who refused to pilot us into harbour, whereby the vessel and all on board were in danger of perishing; but by the kind providence of God we got safe to anchorage, and the man was cashiered for his conduct. But to return to the corporal from the 34th. He carried my boy twelve miles to a village where some of our troops were stationed, and money was collected to pay my coach fare, in addition to which they gave me 2s. for pocket money.

At last I reached my destination, and found the sergeant-major, a son of old William Woffindcn of Batlcy, was just in the act of sending off a letter to me, containing a remittance of £1. I was conducted to the hospital to my husband, and it may easily be conceived how affecting the meeting was, after each had thought the other dead. In about six months, orders were received for his discharge, and he was invalided to the 6th veteran battalion. He remained a while on duty, and was then sent to the Cove of Cork [Cobh, formerly Queenstown] where we embarked for Falmouth. After considerable delay on our journey, we reached Wakefield on the summer fair-day. At Batley we were received by my former friend with the same kind hospitality, his wife greeting me with the affection of a sister.

On the Thursday following, we took a small house in the village, though we had very little in the shape of furniture. A carpenter offered to provide it on credit, but as my husband had not yet obtained employment, we durst not accept the proposal. At length he obtained work, I got a little washing, and was allowed to bring home my food thus earned: so that by degrees we were able to purchase a bed, and a few other articles of furniture. Soon after, our second living son was born. At this time, our cottage, which was indeed a comfortable one, afforded little else but bread and water, for trade was depressed, and my husband frequently out of employment. For seven days we had only seven pounds of bread for four of us.

There are few people whose lives have been as eventful as mine; but the most interesting period of it, and that on which I now look back with the greatest pleasure, is yet to be related. In all my wanderings in foreign countries and my own native land, I had hitherto lived without God in the world: I was ignorant of the Scriptures and of the Lord, the Almighty Creator, in whom we live and move, and have our being. When on my way to Ireland, I chanced to go into a Methodist chapel at Rochdale, where I heard a sermon preached from this text, 'The wages of sin is death'. These words followed me through my future journeyings, and I never could forget them the whole year. I often thought that if ever I reached home again, I would begin to serve my Maker. I mingled among none but carnal people, and so religion was put far from me, but there were seasons when I longed to be with the people of God. On returning to Batley conviction fastened more deeply on my mind. I began to seek for religious instruction by attending the means of grace, and I felt sincerely anxious to renounce sin. The Lord had begun a good work in my heart, for I was dark and ignorant indeed. I could not read the Scriptures, but I had a friend whom I was constantly entreating to read to me. I felt I was a guilty creature, and prayed earnestly to God for pardon of my disobedience. Divine things began to occupy my attention. At first my husband was rather severe with me, and sometimes said he feared I was going out of my mind, for he was a stranger to the God who made him and had preserved him in so many and great perils.

I was very desirous to join a little band of pious persons who assembled at a workshop near our cottage, but my sense of unworthiness was so deep that I was afraid to approach them. On one occasion in particular, I almost resolved to go, but my fears of presuming were great, and most earnestly did I pray that if it were not the will of God He would prevent my going. My husband was seated in the house while I was putting on my bonnet, and I expected he would make some objection; when all at once he exclaimed, 'God has power above the evil one; I intended to hinder thy going, but suddenly these words came into my mind' 'Seek ye first the kingdom of God and His righteousness;!' and from that time forward his resentment against my religious feeling ceased. My knees trembled as I walked along, and when I reached the place, I stood at the door as undeserving an entrance. I found courage at last to enter, and asked one of the members to call upon me, but neglecting to do so, I could wait no longer and so called upon her. The day on which my anxieties about my soul were removed, will ever be esteemed the happiest in my existence. It was on the 8th of February; at about eleven o'clock in the morning. I began to wrestle with God in prayer as soon as I awoke, and resolved that I would not rise from my knees till I had found peace. My cries reached the ear of a merciful God and all at once I seemed as if born again, and the words 'Be thou faithful unto death, and I will give thee a crown of life,' were sensibly impressed on my mind. The witness of the Spirit within me of my acceptance with God was so clear and satisfactory that I could do nothing but sing praise to Him; and the happiness I enjoyed was such as no words can describe. The whole face of nature seemed to assume a new aspect; the very beasts of the field seemed to glorify their bountiful Creator. Great had been the previous distress of my mind, for Satan had often assailed me; but now I feared him not, for God was my refuge. Frequently, even when asleep have I burst forth in songs of praise and thanksgiving.

At first I had not sufficient confidence to approach the theme of grace in fervent supplication in the presence of my husband, but soon obtained it, and I then urged him to join me in this duty. For a while he seemed unwilling to do so, and on one occasion he said he wished I would pray in silence, and not speak so loud as to let the neighbours hear me: but my heart was so full I cared not who knew or heard what God had done for my soul. By degrees his prejudices were removed, and at last, by the goodness of God and His blessing on my entreaties, he was brought to kneel at my side. This was a season ever to be remembered. I love the spot where all this took place, and often regret that I left that happy abode.

But to return to our temporal concerns. Want of work brought us to poverty and much suffering. In the month of June I had a severe illness, that brought me almost to the verge of death, but my heart rejoiced in God my Saviour! Day and night I experienced joy in believing, for my dreams were as full of bliss as my waking thoughts. One night in particular, I had a most impressive vision of the triumphant and exalted King of Glory. My bed of straw often shook under me while I lifted up my voice in holy aspirations to the God of heaven.

My dear William, who was born in December, was put out to nurse, and as my husband was still out of employment, the house was often destitute of a crumb of bread, for all we could spare was sent to the dear babe whose sick mother was unable to nurse it. Still I did not repine nor feel any care, for Christ was mine, and if I possessed nothing else He was sufficient for my soul. The bright views I had of heaven raised me above all earthly trials; so that many of my pious visitors said they envied my situation. The same kind Providence that fed Elijah by means of ravens, has protected me all my life. Friends were raised up to us, and through Divine mercy in the third month I began to recover. My kind partner was very affectionate and attentive to me, and did all he could to make me comfortable, for I could not have any other nurse. As soon as I was able to sit up, Satan tempted me with doubts of God's Providence. The question suggested to me was this, 'Would God thus afflict me if I was His child?' I took up the Testament (having by great diligence learnt to read a little), and read these words, which I had never to my knowledge heard before, 'All things work together for good to them that love God.' When my husband came in, I read the verse to him: he stood astonished and speechless, for he could read his Bible as well. My fears vanished, and peace was restored to my soul: but my bodily strength increased but slowly. A few months after, the same inward disease attacked me, and I had been confined to my bed about a week when my husband was brought home in a sad wounded state. He had been carrying some cloth on his back across a boarded floor, part of which was covered with a sheet that prevented him from seeing there was a large opening, and down he fell the moment he set his foot on it. This was a great affliction, but we were not left to perish. Small sums of money were at different times collected by kind friends, to whom we were very grateful. In a few weeks we were both restored to moderately good health; my husband was enabled to make comfortable provision for his family till the time of the 'Union' when he was without work for twenty-two weeks; and we were reduced to extreme want.

When my next child was born, I had no means of procuring a nurse, and my children were starving around me, but the Lord brought me through this trial. When I was strong enough to go out to wash, I made a practice of taking home the dinner given to me, and sharing it with my husband and children, who would have otherwise had to go without a meal. When this season of poverty had gone by, and comfort was in some measure restored to us we felt more grateful than if we had not suffered such severe privations. Still, affliction left us not altogether: and it was wisely so ordained. For five successive winters my husband had been afflicted more or less with asthma, and he was for a long time unable to work, and when able, not obtaining employment, he managed to bring in a trifle of money by keeping a small school. About six weeks before the illness which terminated his life he obtained the desired employment.

For three quarters of a year, I was in a very precarious state of health. We were also in great distress for want of food: I had often nothing wherewith to satisfy the children, save the sweets exposed for sale in the window. But though thus affected in body, that peace of mind which the world knoweth not was seldom for a moment clouded. Such was the serenity of my mind, that my husband would frequently say 'Thou hast forgotten us.' Never did I more earnestly long to depart to 'fairer worlds on high,' but unerring Wisdom ordained it otherwise, and I am yet spared. But even in times of greatest extremity, and when nothing but starvation seemed to await us, we were still like Elijah of old—the cruse of oil no sooner failed, than more was provided. On one occasion a most unexpected supply of flour, bacon, cheese and potatoes was brought on a very stormy night. The person who befriended us so providentially, was the last to whom I should have looked for assistance; and this additional instance of God's kind providence almost overwhelmed me. 'Oh, my children,' I exclaimed, 'Kneel down and help me to praise the Lord for his mercies.'

We were visited by the ministers and other kind friends, few of whom came empty-handed. Extreme as was our penury, we rejoiced that our crooked places were made straight, and the rough paths smooth. And now another trial awaited me. My dear husband finished his last day's work on Saturday, August 30, 1828. On going in to the chamber where he worked, I found him gasping for breath, and his face as pale as death. I entreated him to leave the cards for me to finish, and said that he should not 'raise' any more, as it seemed to harrass him so much. He attended public worship on the following day, though with difficulty. About three o'clock on Monday morning, I was taken in labour, and he sent for the doctor. This was a distressing day. After the child was born, my husband came in to me, and I at once observed a striking change in his appearance. He was very anxious to continue his work, for our eldest son was unable to assist us, having been ill several weeks. In the course of the evening, the woman who was attending me overheard a neighbour say, 'Poor Catherine, if I thought she was in want, I would send her a shilling.' Soon after I was alarmed by my husband exclaiming 'Oh! send for someone to pray with me, and for the doctor.' My eldest son, weak as he was, was soon sent off; the door was kept open all night, and the casement taken out of the window; this was necessary for his respiration though it might have produced fatal consequences to me. He did indeed seem near his end. I raised myself in bed, extremely agitated. The doctor came to me, and requested me to be as composed as possible, or he could not answer for the result. I almost think he expected to find us both corpses in the morning. About four in the morning, my husband grew a little better, though he was in a state of extreme weakness. For a fortnight he sat in his chair without lying down; but gradually recovered so as to walk a short distance with a stick. I used to watch him the live-long night with a wife's anxiety, the perspiration rolling off his face in heavy drops.

About this time, which was a season of great suffering, our neighbours collected 30s. for us, besides a liberal supply of provisions. As regards my bodily health, the Lord strengthened me wonderfully; though it was my twelfth child, I was able to part with my nurse at the end of the week. For the little while that my dear husband was spared to me before his relapse, he diligently attended to the household affairs, and even undertook the care of our young infant, whilst I employed myself elsewhere during the greater part of the day for the support of our family.

It was on one of those occasions when returning home, with a ghastly countenance he observed that I must go no more, and added, 'I shall not long be here, stay with me so long as the Lord shall spare me.' Some time after, struggling for breath, he remarked, 'I have delivered up all my earthly treasure; Christ has subdued me to His will, and I have almost done with the world.' He again expressed the wish that I would talk to and encourage him, and also requested that I would go to prayer with him. As well as I could, I did so; soon after, his voice which had so often failed him, became at once so powerful that he sang the following lines with great energy:-

'Praise God for what He's done for me!
I once was blind, but now I see.
I on the brink of ruin fell,
Glory to Thee, I'm out of hell!'
'Praise God from whom all blessings flow,' &c *

He continued in the flesh until Sunday, having taken his bed the day before; soon after two p.m. he struggled hard for breath, and requested that some of the pillows might be removed: this desire to lie low was, as I appre-hended, a symptom of approaching dissolution. He then slumbered a little; and his brother and other friends came to take my station at his bedside, and insisted on my lying down to rest. I did so, but not for sleep. When I returned to my husband, I perceived his hour was come. He warmly clasped my hand in his, and added with much feeling, 'May my sweet Jesus be thy comfort.' These were the last words he uttered. I removed the pillow from under his head, which as I lowered he gently expired without a sigh or groan, on the 12th January 1829.

---

* This hymn (*O blessed Lord to thee I pray*) was included in *A Selection of Hymns for the use of the Female Revivalist Methodists*, 1838; 'Praise God from whom all blessings flow' is a standard doxology.

I now felt my situation desolate indeed. For several months I was in a very debilitated state; and my medical attendant will recollect that when he left the village for a short season, on the occasion of his marriage, he had no expectation of seeing me again alive. But the Lord was pleased to raise me up; and considering that my constitution is badly shattered, I have enjoyed as good health as might be expected. I am sometimes disabled from attending to the wants of my family, and am compelled to hire a washerwoman; yet with these and other drawbacks, the Lord never fails to make a way for me: marvellous are His doings! 'My souls shall yet praise him, Who is the health of my countenance and my God.' [*Psalm 42:11*]

And now, kind friends, if anything here written has afforded you any interest, I shall indeed rejoice. What remains of my humble history to the present time—(when I have reached my 78th year)—merely the common every-day occurrences of a quite old age, and therefore not of such importance as to interest the reader. May I have grace given so to live in the flesh that I may one day be joined to my dear husband in the spirit, in that eternity of heavenly rest purchased for us through the blood of our Redeemer, in whom living or dying in pray to be found.

The relatives of Catherine Exley regret having to add that she departed this life the 20th day of April 1857, being in her 79th year. Many a time has she been known to express her desire to see the small work before the public; but just on the eve of its being published (in fact, when it was in the hands of the printer) she has been called away.

The Campaigns of Joshua & Catherine Exley

Prof. Charles Esdaile, University of Liverpool

A COMPREHENSIVE introduction to the causes of the Peninsular War would require a volume to itself, yet in any case the reasons as to why the British found themselves fighting the French in Iberia are not directly relevant to the day-to-day experiences of Catherine and her husband. Very briefly, however, in May of 1808 a decision on the part of Napoleon to overthrow the established governments of Spain and Portugal had led to a serious insurrection against his rule that quickly spread from one end of the Iberian peninsula to the other. Eager to exploit this opportunity, the British government had immediately dispatched an army to Portugal, and there it had continued to operate until the time Joshua and Catherine arrived.[1]

In the British army of the Napoleonic period, the cornerstone of a soldier's life, and for that matter that of a 'camp-follower', was the primary unit to which they were attached, be it the infantry battalion, the cavalry brigade, or the artillery battery, and, Joshua Exley having been a member of the Second Battalion of the Thirty-Fourth Foot, it therefore seems a good idea to begin with a brief account of the organization of the British infantry. Like most infantry regiments then, the Thirty-Fourth Foot was composed of two battalions, each of which consisted of ten companies, of which one designated as a grenadier company and another a 'light' company (i.e., one trained

59

to fight in open order as skirmishers). At full strength, each battalion should have had 1,000 men, but in practice this figure was rarely achieved even when battalions were at home in Britain, and still less so given the manner in which the exigencies of the war against Napoleon had forced the abandonment of the theoretical norm of the first battalion of each regiment being sent to fight the foe whilst the second stayed at home to gather in recruits and function as a training organization. In the case of Joshua Exley's Thirty-Fourth Foot, the First Battalion spent the whole of the Napoleonic period in India, and so it simply may have been judged a lot easier to field the Second Battalion in Spain and Portugal rather than attempt to transport hapless recruits half-way around the world and see large numbers of them perish *en route*. That said, deploying both battalions of a regiment overseas at once was equally problematic, as the result was that the only fall-back was the efforts of recruiting parties sent to tour the British Isles in the hope that they could drum up recruits from either the populace at large or the county militia, the Second Battalion of the Thirty-Fourth (conventionally the '2/34th') clearly being no better off than many other units in this respect. Thus, 996-strong on its arrival in the Peninsula in 1809, at the battle of Buçaco in September, 1810, the battalion is listed as having an effective strength, excluding officers, of 617 men, but at the battle of Albuera in May, 1811, the number was down to 568, while at the battle of the Nivelle in November of 1813 it had fallen to just 452.[2]

Who, meanwhile, were these men? In theory, the Thirty-Fourth Foot was associated with Cumberland: indeed, it bore the title of the Cumberland Regiment, and was nicknamed 'the Cumberland Gentlemen'. In reality, however, this association existed on paper only, the likelihood being that few of either the officers or the men would have had any connection with the county. Privileged by social and economic conditions that were particular to those countries, specifically Scottish infantry regiments recruited almost entirely in Scotland, and specifically Irish ones almost entirely in Ireland, but English regiments such as the Thirty-Fourth Foot were forced to cast their net much wider, sending recruiting parties all over the British Isles and drawing on the manpower of a wide range of militia regiments. (To elucidate a little, during the Napoleonic period recruits—all of them volunteers—came from two sources: men who were recruited directly from the civilian populace, and men who were recruited from the county militia.) As for the army's officers, these, too, came from a wide range of regions and backgrounds, though Scots and, especially, representatives of the Protestant ascendancy, were heavily over-represented (a good example of the latter is George Bell, a young ensign who joined the regiment in 1811 and whose memoirs we shall be making much use of in the course of this chapter). As a result, the Exleys would have found themselves in a world that was extraordinarily polyglot (that said, up to 40% of recruits in the army as a whole were Irish Catholics). If the rank and file were culturally diverse, however, they were socially far more homogeneous. Thus, whilst records of the occupations of the men who joined up are incomplete, it would appear that the largest single category were labourers, and the next largest group handloom weavers, this last being an occupation that was under particularly heavy pressure at this time due to the onset of mechanization in the textile industry. In short, most of Joshua Exley's comrades would have been men from the poorest and most disadvantaged sectors of society, and some of them at least would beyond doubt have been, at best, very rough diamonds: as was widely accepted, every regiment had its share of thugs and common criminals. But outright 'scum of the earth' the men were not, there being plenty of decent individuals of the sort of Joshua Exley who had donned red coats not because they were on the run from the law, but rather because they had fallen on hard times or simply wanted travel and adventure. Indeed, in one or two instances, such was the sustained propaganda war in which Britain was caught up that they might even have wanted to fight for King and Country![3]

So much for the composition and structure of the British infantry. What, though, of the experiences and quality of life of a British infantryman? With the British army then in a state of immense flux in which enlightened theories of training and man-management clashed continually with an older order based on ruthless subordination and the use of the lash, here much depended on the man in command of the individual battalion and, to a lesser extent, his captains and subalterns. In Joshua's battalion, until the Battle of the Pyrenees at least, this was a Lieutenant-Colonel William Fenwick, whom Ensign George Bell describes as 'always kind—an amiable man, a good and gallant soldier, decided in character, just and impartial'.[4] Just as agreeable, meanwhile, was Bell's company commander, Captain Charles Fancourt, Bell describing him as 'a first-rate fellow, a fine and gallant soldier, always generous, hospitable and kind', while another officer of the battalion who will figure in this chapter, namely Joseph Moyle Sherer, later wrote of the rank and file in a manner that clearly suggests that he was at the very least sympathetic towards them.[5] Flogging, alas, was by no means unknown—Bell speaks of witnessing it at first hand on a number of occasions, though it is not quite clear whether the men he saw being flogged actually belonged to the battalion[6]—but on the whole the impression that we have is that the unit was a happy one, or, at the very least, one that was no worse than many in the army. On the whole, then, Joshua Exley may be reckoned to have been quite fortunate.

Whether this was the same for Catherine is another issue. The world of the baggage train in any regiment was beyond doubt one that was at best rough and ready at the best of times, and, whilst there was undoubtedly much kindness and mutual support, this could beyond doubt be mixed with just as much bullying and one-up-woman-ship. Once again, the situation in which the newly-arrived soldier's wife found herself was very much down to luck, and it is for the most part impossible to divine the atmos-phere in any given regiment. Yet Catherine, too, may have been lucky, for the camp followers of the Thirty-Fourth Foot at least possessed a natural leader in the form of the redoubtable Bridget Skiddy. The wife of an Irish soldier named Dan Skiddy who had been taken on as a servant by George Bell, Mrs Skiddy positively explodes from the pages of his account of the war. Physically, she was not very prepossessing: Bell calls her 'a squat little Irish woman, and broad as a big turtle'.[7] Yet what she lacked in looks, she more than made up for in competence, courage and character. To quote Bell again: 'She was a devoted soldier's wife, and a right good one, an excellent forager, and never failed to have something for Dan when we were all starving.'[8] To illustrate this point, meanwhile, we are told a number of moving anecdotes. First of all, there is the picture of 'Mother Skiddy' defying the orders that the camp followers should always march in the rear, insisting on being 'foremost on the line of march' the day after a group of provosts had shot the donkeys belonging to some of her fellows as a punishment for the women having tried to push ahead so as to get things ready for their husbands when they fell out at the end of the day's march.[9] Then there is Mrs Skiddy, complete with her donkey, 'The Queen of Spain', once again defying orders to remain in the rear at the crossing of the River Nive on 8 December 1813, on the grounds that if her husband was killed there would be no-one to bury him.[10] And, finally, there is the Mrs Skiddy who carried her husband on her back for many miles when he collapsed from exhaustion during the terrible retreat to Ciudad Rodrigo in November, 1812.[11]

The idea of Catherine Exley turning to Bridget Skiddy for comfort and support is an attractive one, for over the years that followed such comfort and support were to be much needed (at the same time, being both literate and from a comparatively comfortable background, Catherine was a natural target for bullies). That said, however, Catherine does not seem to have been physically present with the regiment for most the year and a half that followed her arrival in the Peninsula, rather being forced by sickness and pregnancy to remain well behind the lines, for the most part in the vicinity of Lisbon. During this time, however, having been joined by Joshua in the late summer of 1810, the battalion fought in a number of engagements. First of these was the battle of Buçaco of 27 September 1810. Occasioned by Wellington's effort to block the third French attempt to conquer Portugal at a high north-south ridge known as the Serra do Buçaco, east of Coimbra, this resulted in a dramatic French defeat which saw every enemy attack beaten off with heavy losses. However, deployed at the very southern end of Wellington's line with the rest of its parent brigade (that of Catlin Craufurd, the other units which this contained being the 2/28th and the 2/39th) the 'Cumberland Gentleman' did not fire a single shot.[12] To make matters worse, meanwhile, the battalion then had to endure the misery of the long, hard retreat on Lisbon occasioned by the fact that the French commander, the resourceful and determined André Masséna, had found a narrow country road that enabled him to outflank Wellington and threaten his position from the north.[13]

What saved the Anglo-Portuguese army was the presence of the extraordinary complex of defensive positions known as the Lines of Torres Vedras. Stretching across the Lisbon peninsula from coast to coast, these consisted of successive belts of redoubts mounting heavy guns and protected by a whole variety of obstacles including inundations, abattis and artificial scarps. Yet Catherine has nothing to say about any of this—indeed, not having been present with the army during the retreat from Buçaco, she may never even have seen the Lines—while her account of the campaign of 1811 is also at best sketchy. In brief, what transpired insofar as the 2/34th was concerned was that in late February a large force of troops was detached from Wellington's main army under the command of General William Beresford and sent south-eastwards across the River Tagus to march to the relief of the major fortress of Badajoz. Craufurd's (now Abercromby's) brigade being part of a division—to be precise, the Second—that had been attached to Beresford's command, the 2/34th was included in this force, and by late March it was on the frontiers of Extremadura (the Spanish region which adjoins the central part of Portugal's eastern border). Badajoz, it transpired, had already fallen to the enemy, but Beresford's column was able to retake the minor Portuguese outpost of Campo Maior (this is the 'castle' referred to by Catherine on p.27). There followed an attempt to besiege Badajoz, but this had not got very far when the commander of French forces in Andalucía, Marshal Soult, appeared from the direction of Seville with a large army, the result being the battle of Albuera. Of this affair Catherine says very little, and it appears from her memoirs that neither she nor her husband were present, both of them having been detached to the rear to attend the regiment's sick in the hospitals that had been established at the nearby Portuguese fortress of Elvas. As such, we can pass over it very quickly, though it was in truth a terrible affair in which the 2/34th suffered very heavily. Thus, initially positioned in the centre of the defensive line which Beresford established at the village of Albuera to block the road to Badajoz, the Second Division had hastily to be switched to the right flank when Marshal Soult launched an ambitious attempt to envelop Beresford's army from that direction, its three brigades having in effect to be flung into action piecemeal in order to forestall the total collapse which otherwise threatened. In the fighting that followed, Abercromby's brigade was hit rather less hard than its two fellows, but even so its losses were bad enough, the 2/34th's share of the 'butcher's bill' amounting to 128 officers and men killed, wounded and missing.[14]

To return to Catherine's memoir, the passage that follows her very brief mention of the battle of Albuera is very vague, and the only things that can be judged with any certainty are, first, that, albeit from the relative safety of a spell in sick quarters, she and her husband witnessed the stand-off on the River Caya in the summer of 1811, and, second, that in October 1812 they were with the 2/34th when it reached the town of Aranjuez (Catherine's 'Arinjos') after advancing up the Tagus valley from Extremadura in the wake of the French decision to evacuate Andalucía on account of Wellington's victory at Salamanca on 22 July. Presumably the events in between had completely slipped her mind, but, in brief, the Second Division remained in Extremadura when the rest of the British army, which had come down to help retake Badajoz, moved back north to the frontiers of León in the late summer of 1811. It was therefore not involved in the campaign of El Bodón in

September, 1811, but the following month it did take part in the surprise of Arroyomolinos, this seeing an Anglo-Portuguese raiding force take an isolated French division unawares after making a forced march in which it covered some 120 miles through the toughest of countries and the worst possible weather in just five marches.[15] The winter was spent in billets in Mérida (50km east of Badajoz), and, following participation in the covering operations necessitated by the siege of Badajoz, which Wellington resumed in March 1812 (this time successfully—the city was finally stormed on 6 April), in May the Second Division marched to destroy the vital bridge over the River Tagus at Almaraz, though once again the 2/34th were scarcely engaged (along with the rest of its parent brigade, it was sent to launch a preliminary attack on a fort the French had constructed on a mountain overlooking a strategic pass at Miravete some miles to the south, only for the assault to be abandoned as hopeless when the garrison was alerted at the last moment and opened a blaze of fire).[16] Only then did there follow the long march to Aranjuez, this proving to be a place that exhibited plenty of evidence of the horrors of war. Here, for example, is Captain William Webber of the Royal Artillery:

> This is really a melancholy place. The houses are good, the streets broad and regular, and everything that could have been to make [it] worthy [of] a royal residence, and I have no doubt that ten years ago, or even five, it was the summer resort of the first families in the kingdom. But what sad changes and revolutions have there been! Houses deserted, others destroyed, and some inhabited by people dispirited, sickly and suffering the pangs of poverty. Every entrance has been barricaded (by the French) with palisades having loopholes, every wall built higher, and the windows of those houses near the entrance to

the palace have been destroyed and the spaces filled up with bricks cemented in, leaving loopholes only. [17]

To the extent that the 2/34th enjoyed a period of rest and relaxation at Aranjuez, this proved short-lived. Badly shaken by the defeat at Salamanca, in the summer of 1812 the French had been in retreat, with the result that Wellington had been able to liberate Madrid. Thereafter he had launched an offensive in Old Castile which culmi- nated in the siege of the castle of Burgos, whilst leaving behind a large force to rest and recuperate in and around the capital. By the second half of October, however, the invaders had recovered their equilibrium and were moving in the direction of a counter-attack. On 19 October, then, Wellington abandoned the siegeworks at Burgos and started falling back on Salamanca, and at the end of the month the troops in the Tagus valley followed suit. Considerable disorder and drunkenness among the rank and file notwithstanding, the 2/34th and the rest of the forces that had been holding Madrid reached Salamanca in one piece, but thereafter the situation deteriorated alarm- ingly: ordered to retire from Salamanca to the Portuguese frontier, the army was not only assailed by torrential rain, but also for several days deprived of all food thanks to a temporary collapse in its logistical arrangements. Writing fifty years later, Catherine Exley, who at the time was again very sick, remembered the suffering she had endured very clearly, the details that she provides (p.31 onward) being so graphic that they are scarcely worth supplementing. Here, however, is the account that George Bell provides of the night of 6 November and, subsequently, the march under- taken by the battalion the following day:

> The enemy followed and pressed us hard until night, when they bivouacked. We did the same after a good

start in advance. It rained hard and the ground was one great swamp. We had no baggage, it being all in front, as is usual in retreat. I got up into a cork tree amongst the thick branches and balanced myself there until we moved on about four o'clock in the morning. This was a hard day upon the men from the heavy rains. Many fell out, some sick, others disabled and footsore. Hundreds broke down, overcome by the great weight they had to carry in addition to the wet clothes on the back, viz. a knapsack, heavy old flint firelock, sixty rounds of ball cartridge, haversack… wooden canteen, bayonet, greatcoat and blanket – [and] half-choked with a stiff leather girdle bout the throat and as many cross buff belts as would harness a donkey. It is wonderful how they moved along, and more surprising that they were not all left on the line of march. As it was, the French were picking them up in scores as they dotted the cheerless route.[18]

The months of recuperation that followed the retreat to Ciudad Rodrigo ('Radeugo' and 'Therigo' in the *Diary*) are skimmed over by Catherine, and her account does not pick up again until we arrive at the battle of Vitoria of 21 June 1813. In brief, however, what happened over the next few months was that, having received numerous reinforcements, Wellington resolved on a fresh attempt to eject the French from Spain, and, thanks in part to the considerable diversionary effect exerted by the flying columns of Spanish troops—the 'guerrillas' made so much of by the popular British historiography of the war—that had overrun large parts of the Basque provinces, Navarre and Aragón, in May he succeeded in crossing the Portuguese frontier and eventually all but surrounding the bulk of the French forces in Spain in the valley of the River Zadorra just west of the city of Vitoria. There followed the decisive battle of the war. Amongst the first troops to go into action, the 2/34th, 2/28th and 2/39th attacked the village of Subijana de Alava and soon became embroiled in a bitter battle, it being the brigade's advance on this village that Catherine followed at the start of the battle, the many dead and wounded she saw lying by the wayside testifying to the heavy fire that the men endured as they advanced (p.36).[19] Here, once again, is George Bell:

> We were gaining ground along the side of the mountain, when we were met with a biting fire, and the battle here remained stationary for some time until our general sent us more aid. Then… we won the village of Subijana de Alava… and maintained our ground in spite of all opposition. There was a good deal of fighting in the churchyard, and some open graves were soon filled up with double numbers. Churches and churchyards were always a favourite resort for this particular amusement. They were places of strength, and contended for accordingly…. I thought that we had killed more of our French neighbours… than was needful, but, as they cared little for life in their excitement, they would be killed. As Colonel Brown said, 'If you don't kill them, boys, they'll kill you: fire away!'[20]

Also heavily engaged was Joseph Sherer, though his account of the details of the fight is markedly different from that of Bell. Thus:

> My brigade marched upon the village of Subijana de Alava… and had orders to carry it with the bayonet. The enemy opened upon us with fourteen pieces of artillery from their position as we moved down, but with little effect…. Not a soul was in the village, but a wood a few hundred yards to its left and the

ravines above it were filled with French light infantry. I, with my company, was soon engaged in some sharp skirmishing among the ravines, and lost about eleven men killed or wounded. The English do not skirmish as well as the Germans or the French, and it really is hard work to make them preserve their proper extended order, cover themselves, and not throw away their fire, and in the performance of this duty an officer is, I think, far more exposed than in line fighting. I enjoyed, however, from my elevated post, a very fine view of the field.[21]

Fortunately for the 'Cumberland Gentlemen', the advance of substantial Anglo-Portuguese forces across the River Zadorra further to their left gave the defenders of the Subijana sector no option but to retire, the French retreat being so precipitate that Joshua Exley and his comrades never really got back into the battle.[22] Even so, however, at ten men dead and another sixty-six wounded, their losses were serious enough, and the survivors must have hoped for a period of rest. Hardly was the battle over, then, than the Anglo-Portuguese army was advancing deep into the foothills of the Pyrenees, the Second Division taking up blocking positions on the very frontier of France around the passes of Maya (Catherine's 'Myhou') and Ronces-valles, while other forces besieged San Sebastián and Pamplona. Heavy though the French defeat at Vitoria had been, meanwhile, the many enemy troops that had escaped from the field and got away across the border were being regrouped and restored to order under the efficient leadership of Marshal Soult, and on 25 July the French commander launched a massive attack on the troops holding the passes in the hope of breaking through and effecting the relief of Pamplona. As we learn, this was to be a combat that played a decisive role in the story of Joshua and Catherine Exley. As the battle began, the 2/34th and its two fellows were encamped in the valley beneath the Pass of Maya, and, as soon as the alarm was raised, they sprang to arms and rushed to the assistance of the relatively few troops who were actually stationed at the summit, including, not least, a picket from the Cumberlands commanded by none other than Joseph Sherer (having caught sight of French troops climbing the pass from the other side, Sherer and his men put up a good fight, but they were overwhelmed by the enemy's skirmishers, Sherer himself being taken prisoner).[23] Rather than following the winding road that led to the summit, however, the relief force rather elected to take the more direct route up the steep slope that overhung their camps, but the effect of this was to cause the attack to lose all cohesion, and the brigade never got into action as a single whole, but rather made the advance as separate battalions. This was a recipe for disaster. The summit was crowned with at least four battalions of French infantry, with another four in reserve, and these just shot down each unit as soon as it came in range. As it happened, the lead unit was the 2/34th:

> We got away up hill as fast as we could (the men never went on a parade at any time but in heavy marching order, just as if they were never to return to the same spot). But the pass up was narrow, steep and tiresome, the loads heavy and the men blown. We laboured on, but all too late, a forlorn hope: our comrades were all killed, wounded or prisoners. The enemy had full possession of the ground. Some 10,000 men were there… enough of them arranged along the brow to keep us back. It was death to go on against such a host, but it was the order, and on we went to destruction: marking up a narrow pass in file, with men pumped out and breathless, we had

no chance. The Colonel [was] always a good mark, being mounted and foremost: he was first knocked over, very badly wounded. The Captain of Grenadiers (Wyatt), a very fine handsome man, being next in advance, was shot through the head: he never spoke again. My little mess-mate, Phillips, was also killed: I thought at the time, what a sin to kill such a poor boy. Seven more of the officers were wounded, the adjutant, severely hit, tumbled off his horse and was left for dead…. We persevered, pushed on, and made a footing notwithstanding our disadvantage, for the men were desperately enraged and renewed all their exertions to be at them with the bayonet, but in vain. We kept our ground until we were minus in killed and wounded some 300 men and nine officers.[24]

Buckle though the advance eventually did, the 2/34th did not retire from the fight altogether, but fell back to a position a little way down the slope where it formed a firing line and tried to support the equally hopeless attacks made by the other two battalions in the brigade, not to mention a stray battalion of the Fiftieth Foot, but the French were not prepared to put up their efforts and launched a bayonet charge down the slope that soon had the entire unit in panic-stricken flight. It was the end. To quote George Bell once more: 'I never ran so fast in my life…. We were now broken and dispersed…. The old corps was severely handled.'[25] In fact, the situation was not quite as bad as Bell claims—the final casualty figure for the 2/34th was 168 men killed, wounded and missing[26]—but even so it had been a hard day, while, as Catherine narrates, amongst the casualties was her husband, the latter probably having been stunned by a spent ball—this would account for the report that reached Catherine of him having been shot dead—and then over-run by the enemy.

Given that the devastated Catherine now made her way back to England—a decision that says much of her feelings for her husband, most camp followers who found themselves in such a position preferring to stay with their units by immediately taking another husband—the action at Maya brings to a close this account of her experience of the Peninsular War. However, the war was far from over: having taken San Sebastián and repelled a second French counter-offensive, in October of 1813 Wellington invaded France and continued to fight Napoleon's forces until the emperor finally abdicated in April, 1814. As for the 2/34th, it went on to fight in the battles of the River Nivelle and Saint Pierre, as well as being present, though not much engaged, in the battle of Toulouse. More fortunate, perhaps, than many battalions in Wellington's army, its losses in killed and wounded came to seventy-one dead and 272 wounded (in addition, about 100 men were returned as missing at various times, of which at least some must have been killed or wounded, whilst it is probable that deaths from wounds or sickness would have brought the number of officers and men who found a grave in Portugal, Spain or southern France up to some 500. Assuming that the total number of men who served in the 2/34th in the Peninsular War, including officers, came to about 1,600 (a figure that allows for the arrival of up to 500 reinforcements), it can be seen that Joshua Exley was a lucky man indeed.[27]

Aside from heightening our appreciation of what Catherine and her fellow camp followers went through, what this short survey of the battles and campaigns in which she was involved tells us is that, as is only to be expected, Catherine's memoirs are distinctly variable in terms of their quality. Some passages—generally those dealing with episodes of particular intensity—are extremely vivid, yet others are marked by passages of great omission, or simple confusion and muddle (the dates of birth and death of her children being a case in point). This last is especially true in respect of the chronology which is provided for the events of 1812: Catherine's account of the horrors of the retreat to Ciudad Rodrigo are as graphic as anything that was ever written on the subject, whilst its sheer length in comparison with the coverage she gives her experience of the Peninsular War as a whole cannot but be suggestive of the impact which they had upon her, yet the chronology is badly disordered. In all this, of course, her memoirs are not unique, and we are therefore fortunate to have the more detailed and/or immediate accounts penned by Sherer and Bell (though these have their own issues, Sherer being characterised by a strongly Romantic bent and Bell being inclined to a certain degree of exaggeration). What does make Catherine's memoirs unique, however, is their nature and authorship, and the author of this chapter can only lament the fact that they have not seen the light of day until now.

Notes

(Surnames refer to the works in the *Bibliography* on p.150)

1   For full details, see Esdaile, *The Peninsular War.*

2   Oman, *A History*, vol.3 p.545; vol.4 p.631; vol.7 p.537. It seems that when Joshua met Catherine he was part of just such a recruiting party, rather than, as she seems to suggest, serving in the militia (National Archives, WO12/4943, my thanks to Richard Woodhead for this reference).

3   For some recent discussions of the recruitment and social composition of the British army in the period, see Haythornthwaite, *Redcoats*, pp.14-41; Coss, pp.29-85; Linch, pp.56-105.

4   Bell, *Rough Notes* (repr. 1956), p.11.

5   For Bell's views on Captain Fancourt, cf. *ibid.*, p.81.
    Meanwhile, for a statement of views that clearly favour the
    common soldier on the part of Sherer, cf. Sherer, pp.131-2.

6   Cf. Bell, *Rough Notes*, pp.120-1. In this work Bell professes
    himself to be deeply opposed to flogging, but, whilst there is
    no reason to disbelieve him, his ability to have made much
    of a difference in this respect while he was still but a lowly
    ensign must be open to doubt.

7   Bell, *Rough Notes*, p.75.

8   *Ibid.*

9   *Ibid.*

10 *Ibid.*, pp.133-4. Thanks to Bell, we also know the identities of
    two of the other wives who served with the 2/34th, namely
    Biddy Flynn and Betty Wheel.

11 *Ibid.*, p.183.

12 Sherer (pp.111-12) provides a detailed account of the 2/34th's
    part in the action, such as it was, describing how their
    division rushed northwards along the ridge to support the
    centre of Wellington's line, only to arrive just as the attack
    that had been launched against it was recoiling in disorder
    to the foot of the slope. The rest of the day was spent waiting
    for a renewal of the assault, but this never came, the only
    contact with the enemy coming when some soldiers who
    had gone down the slope to get water from a small stream
    encountered some French soldiers bent on exactly the same
    task and had a friendly exchange with them which ended
    with one individual swapping his forage cap for that of an
    enemy infantryman! Sherer's words, however, do provide us
    with an insight into what Joshua Exley must himself have
    seen. As he wrote of the night after the battle: 'The view of
    the enemy's camp far exceeded in grandeur its imposing
    aspect by day. Innumerable and brilliant fires illuminated all
    the country spread below us: while they yet flamed brightly,
    the shadowy figures of men and horses and the glittering
    piles of arms were all visible.... It was long before I could
    tear myself from the contemplation of this scene.'

13 Again Sherer (pp.113-22) provides us with a detailed account of the experiences of the 2/34th as it fell back southwards surrounded by a horde of miserable refugees turned out of their homes by the 'scorched-earth' policy which Wellington imposed on the countryside in an attempt to force Masséna to beat a hasty retreat.

14 For a recent account of the battle of Albuera, see Dempsey. In all, British casualties came to 4,159.

15 Cf. Bell, *Rough Notes*, pp.13-16; Sherer, pp.172-7. A set of French drums captured by the 2/34th may still be seen in the Cumberland Regiment's museum in Carlisle.

16 Cf. Bell, *Rough Notes*, pp.39-40.

17 Wollocombe, p.78. It is worth contrasting this stark description with the much more romantic picture painted by Sherer, who extols (pp.207-11) the faded beauty of Aranjuez's palaces and gardens.

18 Bell, *Rough Notes*, p.72.

19 A survivor of the same cannonade was Ensign William Keep of the 2/28th. Next in line to the 2/34th, this unit also suffered very badly. To quote a letter that Keep wrote to his mother on 8 August: 'Climbing over banks to a village on an eminence called Subijana de Alava, we came within cannon shot of the French. One approach was so open to the range of their guns that we were saluted with a peal of artillery that did immediate execution on a soldier of the Twenty-Eighth and cut his head from his shoulders leaving his body prostrate on the ground before us, unsoiled with blood. Lieutenant Bridgeland, our adjutant stopped a moment to look at him, and, informed by a sergeant of his name, observed that the worst man in the regiment had been the first struck. The same shot took effect upon the shoulder of an officer of the Thirty-Ninth, and his mild and amiable countenance was turned to us without exhibiting any symptoms of suffering, though the wound was too severe a one to hope he could survive long' (cited in Fletcher, p.153). One wonders whether the severed head seen by Catherine

belonged to the man mentioned by Keep.

20 Bell, *Rough Notes*, pp.85-6. As Joshua was then serving in No. 10 Company, he can be assumed to have been in this fight rather than with Sherer's Light Company (National Archives, WO12/4946, my thanks to Richard Woodhead for this reference).

21 Sherer, pp.237-8.

22 A full account of the battle of Vitoria would be too long; briefly, the French were eventually driven from the field with the loss of some 7,500 casualties, all but one of their guns, and the whole of their baggage train. As Catherine implies, the spoil was enormous, but it is not true that 'the wife of Bonaparte' was taken (whether Catherine means Napoleon or Joseph is unclear), the lady in question rather being the wife of General Gazan.

23 Sherer's pickets were not the only men from the 2/34th who were at the summit of the pass when the French attacked; also present was the light company of the battalion: having been encamped with its counterparts from the 2/28th and the 2/39th on the slopes below the pass rather than right down in the valley below, they managed to join Sherer in time to help him try to fight off the oncoming French.

24 Bell, *Rough Notes*, pp.102-3. For the fate of Sherer and his pickets, see Sherer, pp.256-9.

25 Bell, *Rough Notes*, p.104.

26 Oman, vol.4 p.768.

27 The 2/34th's battle casualties have been calculated from the various tables contained in the appendices to the appropriate volumes of Oman. As for the number of deaths from sickness, according to a table in Burnham and McGuigan (p. 234), counting both officers and rank and file the number of British soldiers who were killed in action was 7,595, whereas the number who later succumbed to wounds or disease was 28,015. Consequently, if the 2/34th list of killed in action, including men reported as missing came to 100, it is likely to have lost another 400 deaths in hospital.

In Pursuit of Heavenly Guidance

the religious context of Catherine Exley's life & writings

Naomi Pullin, University of Warwick

Introduction

A S A RECENT Methodist convert nearing the final years of her life, a reminiscent Catherine Exley reflected on her time as an army wife: 'In all my wanderings in foreign countries and my own native land, I had hitherto lived without God in the world: I was ignorant of the Scriptures and of the Lord, the Almighty Creator, in whom we live and move, and have our being.'[1] This penitent declaration highlights the conflict faced by the ageing writer in matters of faith and religion. As a girl, deprived of 'a loving mother', Catherine never received the scriptural or religious instruction that she so greatly laments not having in later life.[2] Yet, despite her self-declared ignorance of a 'Heavenly Guide', Catherine's memoir is nonetheless imbued with a sense of the power of the divine in delivering her through extreme suffering, as well as pronounced emotional and physical hardship.[3] 'The wages of sin is death', she wrote — a powerful expression highlighting fervent religiosity and a desire to place spiritual development above all other material pursuits. Thus, her memoir can be read as a story of suffering and redemption framed within the context of providential deliverance.

This chapter explores the religious context of Catherine Exley's life and writings. In uncovering the unacknowledged story of Catherine's Quaker mother, I will firstly contextualize the experiences of this 'invisible' woman, whose decision to marry a non believer below her social rank ultimately led to excommunication from the social and religious community of her youth. Whilst Catherine senior only had a minimal role in her daughter's upbringing, owing to her premature death, one thing that is striking about this memoir is the powerful providential framework in which many of Catherine's sufferings are described. In comparing the language and experiences detailed in the memoir with the journals penned by itinerant (or travelling) Quaker women, the second section will explore the impact of religious conviction in shaping both Catherine's outlook and the writings of pious women more generally. In addition to contextualising some of the spiritual elements of the memoir, this chapter also contains an overview of some of the records that may facilitate researchers in tracing members of the early Quaker movement.

Catherine's mother and the world of eighteenth-century Quakerism

Little is stated about Catherine Exley's mother in her memoir. We know that her maiden name was Nelson, that she came from a wealthy Quaker (probably merchant) background, and lived in a town called Appleby. This is likely to have been the town of Appleby in Westmorland, which had strong ties to the early Quaker movement (the Society of Friends) and was inhabited by a fairly significant number of Friends.[4] She was disowned by the local Quaker community after she married Catherine's father, who was not only a non-believer, but also from a poorer social background — being described as a comber in the worsted (woollen) business. Dying of consumption when her daughter was only an infant, her premature departure is attributed in the memoir to the isolation and loneliness she suffered as a result of her excommunication. In contextualising this story of disownment, the following section will explore the setting of eighteenth-century Quakerism and delineate some of the reasons as to why the movement took such a firm standpoint against her marriage to Catherine's father.

Living fairly rigid lifestyles, the Quakers' deeply spiritual stance was firmly entrenched within local custom and the outlook of the community. Quakers regarded themselves as a 'peculiar people' and consciously tried to limit their involvement with 'the world', an expression used by the Society to mean people whose values, principles and institutions were viewed to be alien to those of the sect. During the 1670s, the movement established a powerful and highly organized structure of meetings, which developed an effective disciplinary focus. Fearful of the effects that 'pollution' by non members could cause, the system of Preparative, Monthly, Quarterly and Yearly Meetings which emerged across the British Isles ultimately served to admonish members to follow strict public testimonies, or ways of life that separated them from the rest of society. These 'badges of faith', which distinguished members from outsiders, included distinctive plain dress, refusal to defer to social superiors, repudiation of swearing oaths, and rejection of the church tithe.[5]

In addition to formulating a very clear and distinct set of testimonies, Quakers from the earliest days took care to preserve the history of the movement. Early Quakers have therefore left behind detailed meeting minutes, which not only document the lives of their members, but also the rules, disciplines and instructions, as disseminated by the Quaker leadership. Kendal Record Office holds a particularly good collection of extant Quaker Men's and Women's Meeting Minutes dating from the 1680s. No official membership lists were kept before 1837 by Quaker meetings. However, detailed research into the meeting records, particularly the minutes for Westmorland Quarterly Meeting and Strickland Monthly Meeting, which were accountable for the Friends residing in Appleby, would enable a researcher to trace the history of the Nelson family.[6] Their wealthy background would probably have made them active and influential members of the Appleby community and important members of the local meetings. It is therefore highly likely that these records would also include the condemnation and subsequent disownment of Catherine's errant mother in the late eighteenth century.[7]

The increasing impulse of the movement to disown or excommunicate members (like Catherine Exley's mother) who had transgressed its testimonies reflected a general trend towards what has been described as 'retreatism', whereby Quakers decided to withdraw from the world rather than compromise their religious identity and beliefs.[8] Recent surveys have explored the implications of such a hard-line attitude. The American movement, for example, is believed to have disowned about half of its membership between 1750 and 1790.[9] A similar, though less-explored, trend occurred in the English setting as well. A strong focus of the movement's efforts was therefore on the practice of endogamous marriage (marriage with fellow-believers), which was viewed as a safeguard for its survival. Matches between Quakers and non-Quakers were deemed to be contrary to Scripture, and Friends warned that this would result in unhappy alliances between individuals who were 'unequally yoked', or did not share the same spiritual outlook.[10] One leader argued that those Friends who had involved themselves in such 'mixed' marriages had esteemed their 'affections and lusts' above God's Truth.[11] Whilst mechanisms were developed through the Meeting system to try to prevent mixed matches taking place, Catherine's mother clearly placed herself in a precarious position in her decision to go to a priest and marry a non-Quaker below her social rank.

Once the meeting discovered that an unauthorized marriage had taken place, a signed paper of denial, leading to disownment, was jointly issued by the men's and women's monthly meetings. These papers followed a standard format, emphasizing the scandal which the courtship had caused to 'Truth', as well as the hurt caused to the parents of the transgressor and the local community who had advised and admonished against the match. The 'paper of condemnation' read against a Friend from the Strickland Meeting, Dorothy Airey, in 1711, detailed broken promises to her parents and the scandal caused to Friends who had laboured with her to break off the engagement. The paper, which was signed by at least two of her relatives, ultimately declared that 'we can do no less than testifye against all such disorderly proceedings therein, and that we can have no unity and fellowship with her'.[12] The paper of condemnation would then be 'published' through a public reading at the end of a first day (Sunday) meeting for worship at the local meeting house, as well as every monthly meeting where rumours of the transgression had become common knowledge. This public and ritualized shaming practice, highly reminiscent of Anglican procedures of excommunication and penance, suggests that Catherine's mother's decision to join with a non-Quaker was one that would not have been taken lightly. Indeed, it would have been a decision carefully weighed against the obligations of duty to both her parents or guardians and the local Quaker community where she was educated.

It must have been a trying experience for those Friends who were disowned from the Society or who faced scorn from individuals as a result of their transgressive behaviour. Catherine even attributed her mother's death to her disownment. Whilst this is a fairly extreme example, many other Quaker women described a similar sense of loneliness and remorse. After she had left the Society in the early nineteenth century, Mary Wright Sewell of Suffolk declared that she was lonely because 'almost all my friends and acquaintances were Friends'.[13] Indeed, for many women who absented themselves from the movement, or (like Catherine's mother) were forced to withdraw from their local community, they lost not only their Quaker membership, but also their personal relationships, where much of their life was centred. In this respect the remarkable resilience which Catherine's mother demonstrated is certainly a trait inherited by her daughter. For both women the lure of romantic love, so prevalent in this era, may have led them to abandon their former communities and refashion their lives, whether as a Quaker outcast, or a peripatetic 'camp-follower'.

I have painted a fairly bleak picture here of a restrictive movement that stringently policed the lives of its members. However, there were also some positive aspects of eighteenth-century Quakerism which were highly unusual for the time. From its foundations in the 1650s, the Quaker movement was unique in its advocacy of female preaching, where it was argued that men and women had equal access to a God given 'inner spiritual light', because there was no gendered distinction between the souls. This could be an empowering experience for women, who were able to occupy unusually active and public roles as missionaries, preachers and church elders. Perhaps it was this aspect of Quaker beliefs, in its emphasis on the supremacy of individual spiritual revelation that empowered women like Catherine's mother to make independent decisions about their futures. Whilst Catherine never experienced the same deeply spiritual Quaker education, her belated discovery of Methodism clearly influenced how she interpreted her life and circumstances in the memoir. Indeed, it was only through her religious conversion that she was able to acquire the valuable skills of reading and writing — skills which she would have been taught had her mother survived. This also included instruction in the Scriptures.

Confessional tools: the writings of Quaker and Methodist women

Nineteenth-century culture emphasized the importance of the fixed space of the household as a site for female endeavour. Whilst this did not mean that women were totally barred from occupying spaces within the public or political realms, it was unusual for women like Catherine Exley to completely leave their domestic responsibilities behind and adopt itinerant lifestyles. Indeed, like her mother, the decision to leave her life in England behind suggests a courage and daring which few women would have felt able to match at this time. One way in which Catherine attempted to overcome the criticism that might be levelled against her was by explaining her own powerlessness in making such a decision. Her choice of expression, 'I would go in which path soever the Lord directed me', is telling.[14] Catherine's understanding of the divine clearly influenced her perceptions about what she had experienced during the Peninsular Wars. In fact, what is striking about her memoir is how her experiences and sufferings of travel as an army follower during the Peninsular War are framed within the context of providential redemption and deliverance. Some elements of this are highly reminiscent of the language used by itinerant or travelling Quaker women. Guided by the divine spirit within them, they undertook missionary work and recorded their experiences in spiritual journals or autobiographies. In this section, I will therefore explore some of the similarities, as well as evident differences, between Catherine's diary and those Quaker women's writings with which her mother would have been educated.

In highlighting their decision to undertake ministerial service across the Atlantic, Quaker women from the earliest days used similar phrases to draw attention to the uncontrollable force of providence in guiding their travels. Joan Vokins, a minister from the 1680s, and mother of seven children, recounted how during her early spiritual experiences she had 'cried to the righteous God to reveal his way unto me', and had promised 'to walk therein whatever I endured'.[15] Similarly, the American minister Susanna Morris felt justified leaving thirteen children behind, 'believing that the Lord our God required it of me, I dare not wish to have stayed at home'.[16] Both of these women were forced to cede domestic responsibilities to husbands and relatives in their absence. Yet, whilst they had the consent of their families to undertake this work, like Catherine, their writings show a defensiveness about their decision to travel, which they insisted was justified by divine guidance. Indeed, Catherine's narrative is replete with references to the 'Almighty arm', which was guiding her on her travels, even though she had failed to appreciate this at the time.[17]

In addition to divine intervention, Catherine continually makes reference to her own spiritual enlargement in the face of intense trials and bodily weaknesses. She repeatedly emphasizes how she was strengthened by God's providence, in a manner reminiscent of the biblical concept of 'strength in weakness', in which the strength of God was sought to carry the faithful through difficulties.[18] The provision of companions, the care of strangers, and hospitality of neighbours, as well as the emotional strength following her own illnesses and the deaths of her children, are just a few of the examples from Catherine's diary which were used as evidence of divine support. After one illness, which she had believed would prove fatal, she notes how 'the Lord strengthened me, even under such discouraging circumstances'.[19] The Quaker minister Joan Vokins used language of a similar tenor when she explained that 'I have been preserved from great Dangers, Perils by Sea, and Perils by Land [...] but out of them all his mighty Power delivered me, and I am yet alive to magnifie it'.[20] The very existence of a travelling body of women was a direct challenge to the patriarchal norm. Nevertheless, by juxtaposing feminine weakness with the providential deliverances she experienced on her missions, it is clear that, like Catherine, Vokins was able to overcome the pangs of isolation and justify the divine underpinnings of her call to ministry. Like the writings of other pious women, particularly from the Puritan tradition, these texts arguably acted as 'confessional tools', whereby the distress caused by suffering and persecution could have a cathartic effect upon the writer. The Quaker historian Sheila Wright has even suggested that many Quaker women's journals were consciously written to include advice about how best to deal with the conflicting commitments of family and home and the need to serve God.[21]

The struggle which many women faced in balancing their spiritual and temporal concerns had particular significance when it came to converting to a religious denomination against the wishes of a spouse. Indeed Catherine, like many female Quaker converts, faced significant personal and emotional trials as a result of her decision to join the Methodists. The effect which her religious transformation had on family life altered the relationship she had with her husband, Joshua. Out of love, she had been willing to follow him across the battlefields of Europe. But when they were both reunited in Batley, the two failed to see eye-to-eye on religious matters. Catherine described, for example, how her husband 'was rather severe with me, and sometimes said he feared I was going out of my mind'.[22] Another instance she recounted was his wish that she would pray in silence and not speak so loudly that the neighbours would hear.[23] The evident conflict of authority around the issue of whether she was to place obedience to God before her duty to her husband is indicative of the timeless problem of religious conscience. If the husband was an unbeliever, or of a different faith, whom was a wife to obey?

Catherine's challenge over conscience was one faced by many of the early Quaker converts, whose personal relationship with the divine and subsequent call to ministry brought them into conflict with unbelieving spouses. Elizabeth Ashbridge, who converted to Quakerism in the 1750s, documented the conflict that her divine calling posed to her husband's household authority. Following one dispute, Ashbridge explained that, 'as a dutiful wife, I was ready to obey all lawful commands; but when they imposed upon my conscience, I could not obey him'.[24] Her resoluteness in following her spiritual calling, as opposed to her obligations as a 'dutiful' wife, resonates with Catherine's own steadfastness in matters of faith. This is powerfully illustrated through the symbolic act of Catherine putting on her bonnet to go to a local Methodist 'band' meeting for worship, despite the expectation that Joshua 'would make some objection' and thus 'hinder' her departure.[25] Yet, despite their differences, Joshua Exley (paralleling many Quaker husbands) followed his wife's example and converted to the Methodist faith. It was noted, for example, how he had intended to prevent her leaving for the meeting, but was struck by an instance of revelation, which ended his 'resentment against [her] religious feeling'.[26] This tells us something of the important influence which female piety could have on shaping the cultural outlook of the household.

Whilst Catherine was never exposed to the writings or testimonies of women like Elizabeth Ashbridge or Joan Vokins — texts on which her mother would have been instructed from a young age — the similarities between the writings of these Quaker women and the Methodist stance of Catherine's diary are nonetheless worthy of note. One possible explanation for this affinity is the strong association which Quakerism had with the Methodist movement of the nineteenth century. Indeed, it is generally accepted that the declining influence of Quakerism in the late eighteenth and early nineteenth centuries can be attributed to the rise of Methodism, which provided an alternative outlet for disillusioned Friends.[27] The evangelical nature of the movement, combined with internal divisions within eighteenth-century Quakerism, gradually led to the absorption of Quaker converts into this alternative way of life. Nineteenth-century Quakers were also willing to offer Methodist preachers hospitality, money and co operation in the early years of the Methodist revival, which ultimately led to a decline in Quaker numbers. Thus elements of Quaker culture, particularly the independent authority permitted for female converts, continued to permeate the Methodist experience.[28] This not only included an acceptance of female lay preachers, but also a realization of the importance of women like Catherine Exley in the conversion of husbands and the creation of Methodist societies.

The ultimate difference between these women's narratives is that Catherine, as she emphasizes in her memoir, failed to appreciate the deliverances that she had experienced until after she had undergone a religious conversion. One telling phrase is how much she lamented being 'so blind as not to recognize the hand of a protecting Providence under all these wonderful preservations'.[29] Itinerant Quaker ministers often reflected at the beginning of their journals their ignorance of God prior to their conversions. However, unlike Catherine's diary, their journals largely document their post- rather than pre-conversion lives. Thus, at the time of writing their journals, ministers like Joan Vokins and Susanna Morris were fully conscious of the Lord's protecting power and detailed this with cathartic effect in their narratives. Indeed, many of the letters that Quaker women penned to family and friends back home continually highlighted their conscious belief in His providential deliverance, despite undergoing intense emotional and physical trials. In one letter of 1680, which Joan Vokins sent to her husband, she wrote: 'And by this you may all know that my tender God is with me, and carries me through many sore Exercises, and his mighty power enables me to do his Service'.[30] Recognition of divine protection and the Lord's ability to deliver even the weakest of his servants through extreme suffering and persecution served as declarations of faith for seventeenth- and eighteenth-century Friends.

Methodist women, by contrast, never achieved the same independent ministerial status within their movement. Indeed, the preaching efforts of converts like Catherine

Exley would have been very much localized to their own or neighbouring counties, and not to the transatlantic exchanges which characterized the experiences of some eighteenth-century Quaker women preachers. Where this difference becomes most pronounced is in the frequency of spiritual or religious language to describe their journeys. It has been argued, for instance, that Quaker women actively 'marginalized' domestic concerns within their writings, in favour of language with a more deeply spiritual tenor. Hilary Hinds, an authority on the writings of sectarian women in the seventeenth-century, has even suggested that family matters within itinerant Quaker women's journals are only considered 'in an unfavourable comparison with the importance of their spiritual obligations'.[31] Catherine's memoir, by contrast, is filled with references to what can be considered temporal or 'domestic' concerns, particularly in her repeated references to Joshua Exley's welfare, and the births and deaths of their children. It can therefore be suggested that the prominence of these more 'worldly' matters may be owing to the fact that Methodist women were less likely to be absent from their families for extended lengths of time and were thus constantly reminded of their duties and responsibilities within their families. Quaker women's travel journals, on the other hand, tend to subordinate domestic concerns in favour of describing their own spiritual progress and religious development.

Conclusion

It is evident that the loss of her mother at an early age deeply affected Catherine Exley's childhood and adult life. At the start of her memoir, Catherine expressed how she wished for the counsel of a loving mother, someone who would have provided the much-needed spiritual and religious instruction which in later life she so greatly lamented not having had. It is unfortunate that we do not know more about Catherine's mother. Detailed research into the Monthly and Quarterly Meeting Minutes of the Strickland and Westmorland Quakers may yet reveal the condemnation and disownment of a young girl whose surname was Nelson, who married out of the Society and faced censure from both her family and the local Quaker community where she was brought up.

Ties of faith held significant weight within the eighteenth-century Quaker community and ultimately led to the disownment of Catherine's mother. Yet belief in the Lord and his guiding power, as we have seen, could permeate women's experiences across confessional boundaries, whether they were Quakers, Methodists or Anglicans. Catherine's journal, like those of many Quaker women, in some respects acted as a kind of 'confessional tool', whereby her sufferings and trials were presented as illustrations of providential care and the tribulations of faithfulness. Whilst Catherine did not have a religious upbringing or any kind of scriptural instruction, her discovery of Methodism in later life provides an added religious dimension to her memoir. Indeed, as we have seen, the ways in which Catherine frames her experiences of travel, suffering, and salvation occur within a deeply providential context, which can be likened to the experiences of other itinerant and preaching Quaker women. Catherine might not be particularly happy at being linked to a movement which she ultimately blamed for causing her mother's death. But she says at the end of her writings that she would 'rejoice' to think her narrative 'has afforded any interest', and she would surely be gratified to know how this remarkable account has impressed and fascinated such a diverse group of individuals.[32]

Notes

(Surnames refer to the works in the *Bibliography* on p.150)

1   *Diary*, p.50. We know from her memoir that Catherine converted to Methodism and allied herself with the Methodist Meetings for worship prevalent in the North West of England. She notes, for example, how during her journey from Ireland to Batley she was deeply influenced by a preacher at a Methodist Chapel in Rochdale, which encouraged her to 'seek religious instruction'. She later notes how, despite her husband's protestations, she joined with a 'little band of pious persons who assembled at a workshop near our cottage'. Such 'bands' of collective worship, which consisted of homogenous groups of four or five persons of the same sex and marital status, were a characteristic feature of early Methodist organisation, combining what Paul Wesley Chilcote describes as 'intense personal introspection' with 'rigorous mutual confession' (see Chilcote, pp.67–84).

2   *Diary*, p.24.

3   *Ibid.*

4   The rural parishes around Kendal, in particular, were noted for large numbers of Quakers. Population estimates for Cumbria more generally suggest that in 1745 nearly 3% were Quakers (see Burgess). I use the terms 'Society of Friends', 'Friends' and 'Quakers' interchangeably, although in early Quakerism 'Children of the Light' or 'Children of God' were the official terms by which Quakers described themselves—'Quaker' was popularized as a derogatory term by critics, describing the moment when Friends became imbued with the divine spirit and physically trembled or quaked, although some Friends used it without qualification and it is now almost synonymous with the movement. The word 'Friends' was in general use at this time.

5   Frost, p.210.

6   Although lists of members were not compiled officially until
    1837 and the introduction of printed record books, many
    Meetings kept regular lists from 1812. If extant, these are
    contained within the local Meeting records. Appleby did
    not have its own meeting house and is likely to have fallen
    under the supervision of Penrith Preparative Meeting,
    which was one of four Preparative Meetings that made up
    Strickland Monthly Meeting, a constituent of Westmoreland
    Quarterly Meeting. Relevant records are held at Kendal
    Archive Centre.

7   The survival of seventeenth- and eighteenth-century
    certificates of disownment is irregular, as it was not
    compulsory for copies to be recorded by Monthly Meetings,
    but it is highly likely that Catherine's mother's transgression
    and the decision to excommunicate her would have been
    entered into the Women's and Men's Monthly Meeting
    Minute Books once the incident was brought to Friends'
    attention. Research into these records, perhaps beginning
    with the more manageable Women's Minutes, might
    uncover the story of Catherine's mother.

8   Tomes.

9   Levy, p.16. Another estimate suggests that between 1761
    and 1776 the Society disowned close to 1,500 members of
    the Philadelphia Yearly Meeting for 'marriage infractions'
    (Wulf, p.61).

10 This concept of equal yoking had scriptural provenance:
    'Be ye not unequally yoked together with unbelievers: for
    what fellowship hath righteousness with unrighteousness?'
    (2 Corinthians 6:14).

11 Frost, pp.158–9.

12 Kendal Archive Centre, WDFC/F/2 (18A) *Strickland
    Monthly Meeting Testimonies of Disownments, 1706–1780*,
    paper of condemnation issued against Dorathy Arey (*sic*) of
    Strickland Monthly Meeting (3 October 1711).

13 Cited in Wright (2002), p.91.

14 *Diary*, p.31.

15   Vokins, p.16.

16   'Susanna Morris to her Husband and Children' (Sept, 1745), in Bacon, p.75.

17   *Diary*, pp.29, 34, 41.

18   'And he said unto me, My grace is sufficient for thee: for my strength is made perfect in weakness. Most gladly therefore will I rather glory in my infirmities, that the power of Christ may rest upon me. Therefore I take pleasure in infirmities, in reproaches, in necessities, in persecutions, in distresses for Christ's sake: for when I am weak, then I am strong' (2 Corinthians 12:9–10).

19   *Diary*, p.29.

20   Vokins, p.60.

21   Wright (2007), p.100.

22   *Diary*, p.51.

23   *Diary*, p.52.

24   Ashbridge, p.43.

25   *Diary*, p.51.

26   *Ibid.*

27   See Burgess, pp.105–6.

28   Chilcote argues that the sectarian tradition in general, and seventeenth- and eighteenth-century Quakerism in particular, reflected many of the same trends in its acceptance of female ministry and preaching as those of the developing Methodist movement: Chilcote, p.11.

29   *Diary*, p.35.

30   Letter from Joan Vokins to her husband (14 June 1680), in Vokins, p.52.

31   Hinds, pp.175–6.

32   *Diary*, p.58.

Catherine Exley's Cloth & Clothing

Prof. Giorgio Riello, University of Warwick

What did Catherine Look Like?

CATHERINE EXLEY'S autobiography is at first sight a less-than-inspirational document for studying the history of dress and appearances. Like the vast majority of her contemporaries living in the age of revolutions, we do not know what she looked like. There are no photographs of her, even if this medium of portraiture became common towards the end of her life, in the 1850s. She did not belong to the genteel classes that might have aspired to have a portrait painted—not just the conversation pieces of the eighteenth century but also much more mundane paintings. She was not even the type of person who could aspire to a portrait miniature. Notwithstanding the fact that the late eighteenth and early nineteenth centuries abound with representations of social types, and in particular the lower classes—both urban and rural—only rarely can we attribute names to specific portraits. An exception to the rule is Mrs Mee, a gifted miniature portrait painter, almost a contemporary of Catherine Exley, who was not particularly wealthy, though one might wonder how much her own self-portrait was 'aspirational', mimicking the ethereal style of the 1790s through the copious display of muslin, the fashion of the time (Figure 1).

It is much more probable that, in her youth, Catherine Exley would have dressed like the woman in Singleton's painting (Figure 2), wearing a linen bonnet, possibly a striped cotton shawl, a light woollen bodice and skirt, and an apron.[1] Woollens would have been of very common use, especially due to the fact that Catherine had access to the largest area of worsted production in the country. In fact, at the very start of her account, she tells us that 'My father was a comber in the worsted business'. This was not the best job in the industry, as it entailed working with wool soon after it was washed, as part of the preparatory stages. Later, when Catherine returned back to a normal life in the 1810s and 1820s, it seems that her husband Joshua was equally involved in the worsted industry, but possibly in the finishing stages, or more precisely as a simple hand-labourer, as she says that he 'had been carrying some cloth on his back across a boarded floor, part of which was covered with a sheet that prevented him from seeing there was a large opening, and down he fell the moment he set his foot on it'.

One might conjecture that Catherine was totally unremarkable as a young woman in Yorkshire in the 1790s. Had she been more interested in mundane affairs, she might have remarked upon the fact that in her teens fabrics were becoming cheap, and that young women of her generation especially found a new way to be fashionable in cotton.[2] Yet, as for most people living through the period that we define as the Industrial Revolution, Catherine does not mention either the industrialisation and mechanisation of textile production, nor the major changes in textiles and dress that it produced. It is likely however that she would have adopted a slimmer silhouette, probably a derivation of the one-piece demi-robe, with the high waistline that became fashionable in the 1790s, and which represented a big shift in women's fashion that became popular first in France and then in the rest of Europe, and which by the end of the 1790s was changing styles of dress in rural locations (Figure 3). This is conjecture, in the sense that our interest in Catherine is not due to her capacity to exemplify general trends—the ordinary—but her quite extraordinary experience as an army wife in Spain, Portugal and Ireland. And here we move from a history of fashion to one of the deep meaning associated with cloth and clothing.[3] Rather than being interested in a history of appearances, the method here is more anthropological, in the sense that in Catherine's narrative both cloth and clothing are not just material objects but props through which to convey wider concerns. I wish to show how she used cloth and clothing in three different ways: first to reinforce a story of deprivation and degradation; second to mark a narrative of action and agency in adversity—especially as it concerns boots; and finally as a marker of identity and identification.

Cloth and Deprivation

The problem for Catherine was not about being fashionable but about how to stay dry. We know the dangers of pneumonia from Jane Austen's characters, who seem to be developing a chill every time they go out. But in Catherine's case it doesn't rain—it pours:

> I remained about three months with the regiment where it then lay. We suffered many hardships from the inclement state of the weather. The luxury of dry clothing was very seldom known. I usually sat (for it would have been almost certain death to lie down) with my boy on my knee, the waters pouring down from the sky and mountain with extreme rapidity and without cessation.

And then in Ireland:

> I proceeded next morning with my clothes still wet
> on my back, having had no opportunity of drying
> them in my cold comfortless lodgings.

We must remember that Catherine belonged to the first
generation for which water and bathing had some positive
connotations. But Catherine here tells us that she has no
choice: there is no place to shelter herself and her child,
and she clearly does not have a change of clothing. She was
also continually on the move, rendering the situation not
just personally but also physically painful:

> The rain poured down the whole way, and the road
> was so bad that we walked above the knees in mire
> and wet. The sand got amongst my clothes, which,
> rubbing against my body, caused acute pain in
> walking. In this state, we encamped for the night.

The physical challenge caused by continuous movement
did not just result in short-term discomfort—though
Catherine rarely mentions any sun in Spain—but also in
a long-term descent into a condition of hopelessness that
is embodied by dirt, the kind of soiling of clothing that
stands for the deeper challenges of inner self in the face of
adversity.

Her narration stands in stark contrast with contemporary views of 'camp scenes' published exactly at the same
time, in which the world of the British military camp is
represented in vignettes reminiscent of bucolic scenes and
in which order, calm and harmony reign and in which,
of course, there is no vermin and linen is washed by the
wives.[4] Catherine instead shows the material degradation
both of herself and of her husband, a fact that started to be
registered by public opinion back at home:

For 28 days a few biscuits were my only nourishment; my clothes were covered with filth and vermin from having been six weeks without a change of linen.

And she continues:

I need not dwell on our feelings of joy and delight at meeting together after such a period of fearful suspense and extreme suffering. His appearance was truly deplorable. I found him in the guard room, with his clothes in a most ragged state, and comfortless in the extreme.

She uses the concept of 'comfort' in a way slightly different from ours. A concept first invented in the eighteenth century, comfort was not just about physical well-being but designated also a state of moral fulfilment.[5] Catherine later recounted that on arrival at 'Catelas' (i.e., Casas de Don Gómez): 'Here we had an opportunity of purchasing every necessary, providing fresh clothing, and making ourselves tolerably comfortable.' This idea of comfort that is both material and moral is splendidly illustrated by the artist George Morland's 'The Comforts of Industry' and 'The Misery of Idleness', in which financial decline is associated with moral corruption (Figure 4). For Catherine and her husband such a descent was even worse, because it was not their own fault.

The Agency of Cloth

The discomforts and desperate circumstances in which Catherine found herself were clearly marked by her clothing, her linen and general hygiene. Yet, she equally uses textiles to mark moments of unexpected change in her circumstances. In at least two cases she received new clothing, the first time in Spain:

On the ninth day we marched back to Roncosvalles, where we were to remain until we received a fresh supply of clothing. The colonel presented me with £1, and the officers generally contributed two dollars each....

And then at arrival in Portsmouth where she—but not the woman she travelled with—received clothing:

My companion met with a severe disappointment; she, like myself, was compelled to throw her old clothes overboard, but was not so fortunate in obtaining new apparel.

Charity in the form of clothing was not uncommon, and indeed the parish poor received yearly supplies of clothing from the overseers.[6] But in Catherine's case, clothing was as much the material expression of an act of kindness as a medium of exchange. In Spain she didn't hesitate in 'converting' a coarse cloth sheet that she had bought for her husband's corpse into 'articles of dress'. In Ireland, by contrast, she recounts how she made a tactical error: 'Unfortunately, I allowed the sergeant, who was proceeding to Dublin by coach, to take my clothes along with him, some of which I ought to have retained by me to pay my way.' As we know from the scholarship of Beverly Lemire, the most common and easily pawned item in this period was clothing.[7]

Cloth and clothing was sometimes a worry and sometimes a clear asset for Catherine. There was one item of clothing in particular that seems to have had the utmost importance: footwear. Catherine recalls how after a battle 'We stripped the French of everything they had—baggage, ammunition, boots, money, etc.' It is important that the list includes boots, as the ability to walk was fundamental for survival. Catherine narrates extremely long foot-marches, keeping pace with the regular army. She recounts how 'In going down the hills, which were very steep and slippery, we were exposed to great danger, and were compelled to take off our shoes and walk barefoot,' a scene that Rowlandson captures in one of his satires (Figure 5).

Catherine was quite happy to be able to use regimental boots, effectively the only way for her to move:

> When the alarm was given I was putting on a pair of regimental shoes belonging to my husband, having previously thrown aside a pair of worn-out boots, which had never been taken off since the first day of wearing, about three months before.

These would have not been like the Hessian or Wellingtons that we normally see in portraits: the soldier's ankle-boot resembled the low-cut labourer's wooden-soled clog or thick hobnailed boot. In fact Catherine might have not been aware that the boots she now wore were at the centre of a scandal back in England. This was because, despite the British army's large annual spending on footwear, which reached £150,000 in the early nineteenth century, some of the soldiers' shoes fell apart after just one day's march: unscrupulous contractors had inserted heavy clay between the soles of their boots to make them seem sturdier. Newspapers remarked upon the ignominious scene of soldiers disembarking at Portsmouth, who 'dragged themselves along the quay on lacerated, festering, rag-bandaged feet'.[8] In 1810 this moved the engineer Isambard Brunel (father of the more famous engineer Isambard Kingdom Brunel) to establish a factory where he produced army boots through mechanized procedures and by employing veterans.[9]

Identity and Identification

I would like to conclude with two of the most important moments in Catherine Exley's life, both of which seem to revolve around clothing. The first is the presumed death of her husband, in which she identifies a body as that of her husband after examining his clothing:

> After turning over several of the bodies we found that of a corporal in the very place where it had been said my husband met his death. On examining his clothing I thought I knew it, and cried out, 'He is here', but there was no appearance of the mark on his finger; otherwise, I should have been convinced of his identity.

What turns out to be a case of a mistaken corpse is a good reminder that clothing was seen as part of the very identity of people. Run-aways, robbers and—in the Americas—slaves were always described through their physical attributes but also their clothing. Clothing in this sense was a way of identification of people rather than the expression of identity. We find at the very end of her narrative the resurrected husband in the act of disagreeing with her newly discovered religious fervour:

> My husband was seated in the house while I was putting on my bonnet, and I expected he would make some objection; when all at once he exclaimed, 'God has power above the evil one; I intended to hinder thy going, but suddenly these words came into my mind'.

It is a scene in which for the first time we have a precise item of clothing mentioned. The bonnet stands for the head, and indeed it is a coded message to the reader that she had already made up her mind to go out (and therefore needed a bonnet), that she had made a choice, the first important choice of her life. She was no longer a victim (not quite a fashion victim though!), but a woman who had found her way and had a bonnet to go with it.

Notes

(Surnames refer to the works in the *Bibliography* on p.150)

1   For an analysis of this painting see Styles (2003) and (2007).
2   Riello (2013), ch.9.
3   For an example of this methodology see Grassby.
4   See Pyne's *'Camp Scenes'*, National Army Museum 1967-05-12.
5   See Crowley (1999) and (2001).
6   King.
7   Lemire.
8   Matthews, p.119.
9   Riello (2006), pp.232-34.

Figure 1. Self-portrait miniature of Anne Mee (née Foldsone) (1765-1851), c. 1795. Courtesy of the V&A (P.12-1962). Anna lost her father when young and took to miniature painting to support her mother and her many siblings.

Figure 2 (above). Henry Singleton (1766–1839), *At the Inn Door*
(pre-1792). Courtesy of the V&A, bequeathed by Henry Spencer
Ashbee (1834-1900).

Figure 3 (right). *The Fashions of the Day, or Time Past and
Time Present*, satirical cartoon by George Moutard Woodward,
London (published by Walker, 1807). The print shows a
woman from 1740 in 'a Ladys full dress of Bombazeen' (dark
and modest), contrasted with a woman from 1807 in 'a Ladys
undress of Bum-be-seen' (light, revealing, and diaphanous).
Courtesy of the Library of Congress (LC-USZ62-59625).

The Year (1740) a Lady in full dress of _Bombazen_ ——— The Year (1807) a Lady in dress of _Bum-ba-zeen_.

THE FASHIONS OF THE DAY or Time, Past and Present.

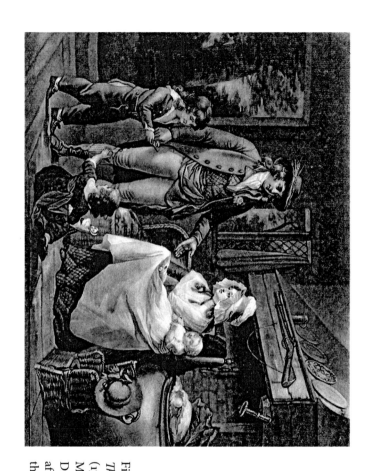

Figure 4a. George Morland,
The Comforts of Industry
(1790). Courtesy of the British
Museum, Prints & Drawings
Department (1873 0510.2609),
after an oil on canvas, now at
the Scottish National Gallery.

Figure 4b. George Morland, *The Miseries of Idleness* (1790). Courtesy of the British Museum, Prints & Drawings Department (1873 0510.2608), After an oil on canvas, now at the Scottish National Gallery.

Figure 5. *Soldiers on a March* (detail). Coloured etching by George Moutard Woodward after Thomas Rowlandson (1811). This caricature depicts men of the 3rd (The East Kent) Regiment of Foot (The Buffs) on the march with their women and children. Anne S. K. Brown Military Collection, Brown University Library.

The Missing Spouse

THE WIVES OF BRITISH PRISONERS OF WAR IN NAPOLEONIC FRANCE: THEIR LIVES & WRITINGS

Elodie Duché

Introduction: the mark of loss

JULY 1813, Basque Provinces. Wending through the bodies of fallen redcoats in the valleys of Vitoria, Catherine Exley was in pursuit of a mark, a banal yet crucial scar on her husband's finger to identify him amongst the dead. For several days and despite the surrounding morbid squalor, she sought his remains, gleaning information from rumours, perusing clothes and corpses darkened by the smoke of cannons and muskets. Unsuccessful in her quest, she bought a 'coarse cloth sheet' in the hope of a future burial before embarking, bereft, on a passage to England; unaware that Joshua Exley, far from being dead, had been captured by the French. Indeed, only several weeks later, upon her return to Yorkshire, a letter from France was to disclose his fate as a prisoner of war.[1] On the whole, Catherine Exley's diary conjures up a vivid and poignant image of loss, the loss of a husband, whose unknown captivity constituted a limbo between life and death. Her diary thus bears witness to the complicated circulation of intelligence in a 'total war' involving civilians and soldiers, men and women, home and front.[2]

This chapter contextualizes this rare testimony by a prisoner's wife, whose diary unravels what could be termed a twofold 'narrative of omission'.³ My intention is first to further explore the silences about her husband's confinement: nine months of detention about which little is stated, except that he was 'tolerably comfortable'.⁴ Whilst tracing his individual 'forced journey' through France remains arduous—his name being absent from the lists available in Kew, Greenwich and Vincennes—one can however retrieve his time across the Channel by using other French sources and life-accounts penned by British captives.⁵ Conversely, by providing a rare insight into how spouses experienced captivity, Catherine Exley's diary fills a void in the story of British prisoners' wives, whose influences are still neglected, if not evicted from conventional narratives of military imprisonment. Indeed, her trajectory resonates with that of other British women, who shared more or less directly the fate of their captive kin. Migration, petition, religion: these are the three main areas the second section will explore to position Catherine Exley amongst other British wives, who occasionally embraced the oxymoronic status of voluntary captives. Ultimately, her journal uncovers a little–documented facet of Napoleonic detention, as it was narrated by female relatives. The final part will thus emphasize how her writings throw into relief not only the place of women in Napoleonic conflicts, but also gendered modes of voicing loss and displacement.

From the 'French Siberia' to the 'feather bed' in Bordeaux: retrieving Joshua Exley's detention

'Englishmen are much the same, whether prisoners or at home', noted Georges Call whilst passing through a French prison-town in 1810, 'playing, driving and shooting at each other. One might fancy oneself in London!'⁶ As a small yet diplomatically valuable community, Napoleon's 15,000 British captives were indeed treated as 'first-class prisoners'.[7] They formed a 'motley assemblage' composed of non-belligerents (mostly tradesmen and genteel tourists arrested as civil hostages in May 1803 with their families) and Navy, Field Army and East India Company servicemen taken under arms in the various theatres of a global war.[8] Under the dual surveillance of the police and army, they were kept somewhat liberally in a constellation of prison-towns, or *dépots* as they were known, in North-Eastern France, yet as far away from salt water as to hinder any attempt at escape. Such leniency was the result of a disparity: the number of French prisoners in British hulks and camps was ten times greater.[9] Paris thus aimed at a reciprocity of treatment between French and British prisoners, whilst adhering to Revolutionary principles precluding ransoming and limiting exchanges.[10]

Variations in the captives' conditions of life were nevertheless significant, depending on their socio-professional status and the context of war. Only those regarded as *personnes de qualité*, that is to say officers and gentlemen, were put on their parole. These captives were simply constrained to remain on the French territory through an 'oath of honour', by which they swore not to escape and could live amongst the locals.[11] In Verdun, they turned the town into a British enclave.[12] Horse-races, fox hunting, whist clubs and amateur dramatics were organized by these privileged detainees, who were nonetheless conscious of the increasingly less fortunate lot of common sailors and soldiers sent to citadels, such as Givet, Valenciennes or Bitche (a disciplinary depot notoriously known as 'the Castle of Tears').[13] The French government granting only meagre allowances, the captives' debts accumulated, which prompted the creation of a Charitable Committee based on a transnational financial network involving the Lloyds Patriotic Fund in London. With ramifications in each detention place, the network led to the establishment of schools and churches, progressively forming a captive diaspora over a decade of imprisonment.[14]

Joshua Exley joined these captive consociates at the twilight of their detention, when the looming tide of invasion from the East, after the Russian campaigns and the battle of Leipzig, led to a hasty redistribution of prisoners fanning out towards the South West. The 'Gurt prison' Catherine Exley mentioned is certainly a phonetic transcription of Guéret, a remote town in the Creuse *département*, where the British captives were gathered in the winter of 1813.[15] Life in Guéret is little documented, due to the confusion surrounding the policing of prisoners, at a time when the priority was clearly more to contain the advance of the Allied forces. Police records and memoirs suggest that it was an impoverished town of 3,500 inhabitants, with a rather inhospitable climate which had forged its reputation as the 'French Siberia'.[16] Joshua Exley would have initially been confined in the *Couvent des Augustins*.[17] Confinement in convents was common practice in post-Revolutionary France, monasteries having been dissolved in 1793 and the buildings abandoned for secular usage. Arguably, living in such an environment could have furthered the tepid nature of Joshua Exley's religiosity, which his wife somewhat resented after his return.[18] Yet, owing to a lack of space, captives were soon billeted on the villagers. The penitentiary ties between captives and captors hence wore away. 'Little or no watch was kept upon us', wrote Captain Langton.[19] Summoned only once a week, certain detainees perambulated in the region in search of fishing sites, others smoked away their ennui in clubs and cabarets. Upon the whole, it was indeed 'tolerably comfortable'.²⁰ The wealthiest fared rather well; hiring country houses and undertaking ethnographic tours to study the 'semi-savage' manners of the locals.²¹

Whilst 'the privations of a prison' lamented by Catherine Exley are thus to be put in perspective, her depiction of a chaotic road back to freedom appears insightful.²² Indeed, the announcement of the fall of Paris on 30 March 1814 resulted in an outburst of joy, leaving 'scarcely a pane of glass… unbroken in the town'.²³ Lord Blayney offered his patronage in Guéret, and secured funds and clothing from local merchants to relieve his subordinates. However, they 'mostly drank out the money and sold the shoes'.²⁴ Some took French leave, others ventured to Paris. Bordeaux was the nearest harbour, yet this was still three hundred kilometres away. The march was gruelling, particularly for poorly-shod and certainly inebriated men who, like Joshua Exley, experienced physical trauma. In his memoir, John Tregerthern Short estimated that between his capture at Dieppe in 1804 and his arrival in Bordeaux in 1814, he had marched '1,276 miles' through France. Bordeaux, then occupied by Wellington, was idealized in prisoners' writings as a foretaste of 'dear England'. Indeed, if Joshua informed Catherine of being 'sumptuously entertained in a kind gentleman's family', his case was not uncommon.²⁵ John Tregerthern Short vaunted of receiving a similar welcome from two 'old ladies', who offered him 'bread, cheese, salad and wine' and 'a good bed'.²⁶

Whilst Joshua Exley was sent to Ireland after a month of convalescence yet still suffering from 'a shock to his constitution from which he never quite recovered', the return home proved equally problematic for other prisoners who had spent a decade in captivity.²⁷ The civil marriage records (*registres d'état civil*) in each depots show that hundreds of them had married French women.²⁸ Others had formed households abroad with their British wives and children. The latter experienced conflicting feelings in returning to Britain, a home they might have not seen before. The daughter of Captain Rainsford of the second regiment of Life Guards voiced these emotions in recollecting her passage from Calais to Dover in 1814:

> There I first saw the sea. My Father took me to walk on the sands and I was charmed with the small corals and shells and the fisherwomen. He pointed out to me where England was… we had a long rough passage, and arrived very sick and wretched at Dover. Everything looked so dreary there and most of us wished ourselves back to France. My little brother exclaiming 'Is this England? Oh! Take me back to France!'[29]

This problematic sense of home strongly resonates with Catherine Exley's experience of displacement and that of other British women missing a captive spouse.[30]

Female trajectories: the 'absent presence'
of British women in captivity

As the French historian Fabien Théofilakis has argued, captivity misleadingly appears as an essentially masculine space, 'a state of radical deprivation, forbidding any female presence'.[31] Until recently, this pre-conception led researchers to neglect the impact of women on captivity, whether directly or indirectly.[32] Catherine Exley's text proves extremely valuable in this respect, by suggesting how women significantly coloured the experience of imprisonment of their male relatives during the Napoleonic era.

Catherine Exley's position falls into what the French historian Sylvie Aprile categorizes as *'l'épouse'* (the wife who stays in the home country), as opposed to *'l'exilée'* (the captured expatriate) and '*la suiveuse*' (the follower joining her captive husband) who experienced military detention at first hand.[33] Indeed, other women featured amongst the victims of the mass arrest in 1803of all British subjects then on French soil. Either lone aristocratic exiles, genteel spouses on their Grand Tour, tradesman's wives or nieces, servants or Indian slaves, these female 'hostages' were exempt from the daily roll-call. Yet they shared the same fate as the male *détenus*. They struggled to receive allowances from the French State, as evidenced by couples' petitions for subsistence in February 1804.[34] Whilst the French secret police records counted ninety-nine British women in Verdun in 1805, their story remains that of an evanescent presence difficult to grasp in the archives.[35] What appears certain is that these female detainees cemented the community of captives abroad, by enabling the recreation of a home-away-from-home. They 'managed matters', i.e. the financial and domestic maintenance of the household.[36] Moreover, they ensured sociability, as exemplified by the active 'social politics' of genteel women such as Mrs Clive and Mrs Clarke who attended clubs, balls and races held in parole depots.[37]

On the other hand, from 1804, other British women migrated to France to join their male relatives, hence obtaining the ambivalent position of voluntary captives. Under the request of their husbands, wives of tradesmen and navy officers in particular, obtained the approval from French authorities, who 'tolerated' their presence in depots.[38] Out of love, financial or religious concerns, others initiated their passage to France without any prior authorisation from alien offices, or even the consent of their husband, as in the case of Mrs Eckford, the wife of a marine officer who 'was quite surprised' by her visit.[39] The case of Mrs Eckford reveals the agency these women displayed in navigating the police system in Holland and France to reach their destination. Like Catherine Exley, she travelled with a female companion and negotiated the patriarchal structure by invoking charity and the hospitality of strangers. Between 1804 and 1811, she travelled three times between Morlaix and Plymouth, both with and without documentation.[40] Her case was not isolated, for in June 1809, a decree was ordered by Napoleon to send all 'Englishwomen and children under the age of twelve, who did not serve as ship's boys' to Brittany to be shipped back to Britain; a measure which met with little success.[41] On the whole, these migrations suggest the great adaptability of couples separated by captivity during the Napoleonic Wars, reinforcing the idea that, for these historical actors, matrimony and family formed less a fixed than a geographically flexible space. The travels of Catherine Exley, presented in *The Dewsbury Reporter* as an atypically adventurous 'Batley woman', suggests that it was perhaps even more the case for the wives of captive redcoats and bluecoats, who were accustomed to recurrent displacement and separation with their husbands, a situation which arguably stood in sharp contrast with the domestic quotidian of other Georgian women of their locality.[42]

Furthermore, in their journeys, British wives clandestinely carried letters and objects, which helped the prisoners circumvent the censorship. 'I very gladly take my pen to embrace the present opportunity of writing unto you which is by way of some English women who have got their passports to return to England', wrote Captain Lelean in 1809.[43] This complicates the common misconception that letters were simply intercepted or lost during the Continental blockade. The diary of Catherine Exley clearly demonstrates how, by being read collectively, as when

Catherine returned to Batley, these letters transformed the prisoners' families, friends and neighbours into 'communities of intelligence'.[44] By petitioning relevant authorities at home, or in the case of Catherine Exley, by informing a 'colonel, who had not then received the returns from France, and was therefore ignorant of [her] husband's situation', women engaged in networks of information and direct political contact with the authorities they wished to influence. They were 'incorporated wives' who acted, if not on a same footing with their husbands, at least in an active partnership with them to alleviate their conditions of detention and ensure their career prospects.[45]

Finally, the letter in itself could further the spirituality of wives missing a captive spouse at home. In this respect, Catherine Exley's growing religiosity resonates with that of other devout women, such as Catherine Lelean, the Methodist wife of a merchant captain from a modest family of shipbuilders in Mevagissey, Cornwall. In the same way as Catherine Exley, she struggled to find means to financially sustain herself and the family in absence of her husband. She resorted to run a Methodist school for local children, which, combined with an active correspondence with her missing husband, furthered her faith. Often received with belatedness, the letter, as an object, materialized the 'absent presence' of spouses separated by the impact of war. Indeed, letters were not merely informative and useful in developing her literacy, but became vectors of a mystical connection beyond captivity, a prayer celebrating a spiritual union beyond temporal concerns. In October 1809, she wrote: 'When I consider the long absence and distance that we are from each other I feel much but tho we are absent in the Body I trust we are present at the throne of Grace. There we find a sweet submission to all the dispensation of his Providence awareness in all things [*sic*]'.[46] If her husband responded with equal spiritual fervour—his letters being read at the local chapel—Catherine Exley's story differs slightly. Her situation reveals that a religious asymmetry could also grow between spouses after displacement. Indeed, after the joys of reunion, Catherine resented Joshua for being 'a stranger to the God who made him and had preserved him in so many and great perils'.[47] It seems that her separation from him may have lessened rather than strengthened the ties between them, especially after her conversion later in her life.[48] Captivity hence proved to be a catalyst, elevating or lessening faith, forging or eroding bonds. This catalyst experience materialized in the *form* and *act* of writing the diary.

The revelation of a letter: Napoleonic confinement, religion and gendered modes of Self-portraiture

'There are few people whose lives have been as eventful as mine…. What remains of my humble history to the present time—(when I have reached my 78th year)… [is] not of such importance as to interest the reader'.[49] Having followed Wellington's regiments in Spain and Ireland, Catherine Exley legitimated the writing of her life, or more precisely one part of her life—her itinerant youth—through the *events* she had experienced. The idea of a *uniquely* 'eventful' segment of life, about which the pious widow was reminiscing in her twilight years, is a trope to be found in other narratives of the period. Her diary is hence characteristic of a post-1789 historical consciousness, where the act of witnessing political and military crises engrained the individual story into the unfolding of History.[50] Yet, what Philippe Lejeune terms the 'autobiographical pact' is complicated by singular gaps and inconsistencies in her text, which only briefly alludes to her husband's detention.[51] Like Fabrice's confused vision of Waterloo in Stendhal's novel *La Chartreuse de Parme*, her narrative thus reveals the multifaceted perception of war by individuals who would only have access to fragments of information.[52]

This confusion raises myriad questions, which archives could partially answer. Yet, I would argue that in all its unanswered questions, its silences, the diary tells us something about the experience of writing the Self. Situated amongst other female trajectories, the itinerary and writings of Catherine Exley suggest that it is then perhaps the purpose of a diary—a published diary in particular—to collect the pieces of a puzzle, where experience and narration are intertwined to make sense of a traumatic moment. Considered through a linguistic lens, the narration appears fragmented by conflicting tenses, superposing the past of the protagonist (the young itinerant Catherine) with the explanatory voice of a narrator (the old Methodist widow), who informs the reader of a capture not yet unveiled to the central character.[53] If this is the product of a retrospective writing inherent to the genre, it is my contention that the diary is also indicative of a particular psychological and spiritual journey, which makes her autobiography not merely a gendered form, but also, an *act*.[54]

Why writing? Why *not writing* about nine months of detention except in a couple of elusive lines? And why did she 'express [a] desire to see the small work before the public'? These questions find partial answers in the narrative patterns of Catherine Exley's prose. The writing of her life was clearly entrenched in a devotional practice she developed later in her life, despite the disapproval of her husband. Through the use of a Gothic language expressing her loss on a fetid battlefield and the physical ordeal of a journey, or pilgrimage, cadenced by multiple deaths and made barefoot with her 'child on [her] back'—somewhat reminiscent of the Passion, her text is permeated by two main biblical features: an end-oriented system of revelation and patterns of recurrence; which, as the Victorianist Heather Henderson has argued, enabled Victorian autobiographers to 'shape their Selves into a larger framework' of historical and religious significance.[55] In this framework, captivity was almost a *non*-event compared to Catherine Exley's progressive yet dramatic discovery of Joshua's survival, forming a pattern of revelation in which *she* was to play the central role. 'I exclaimed "Oh that I too was in France, and a prisoner!"', she wrote, accentuating her position in the disclosure of her husband's lot. This revelation motif culminates in the end of the text where, now widowed and on her death bed, she wished for a heavenly ascension and her story of conversion to be revealed to a broader audience. The way Catherine Exley portrayed herself, in a narration of female suffering forty years after the events she chronicled, suggests that a 'comfortable' detention in Napoleonic France might not have corresponded to her authorial intentions. The diary seems to have been conceived to inspire pathos, piety and a cathartic experience to its readers, perhaps explaining the ellipsis about Joshua's time in France in the first place.[56]

Conversely, if Catherine Exley used the common discourse of uniqueness of experience, her narrative enterprise differs from the larger corpus of memoirs produced by male captives after their liberation. If male authors mostly used their memoir as a justification, defending their honour despite escapes or a debonair life in confinement, as a means to re-enter British society after 1814; Catherine Exley's belated account is a broader introspection through which a multiple subject unfolds. Male detainees' accounts rarely began with a social and religious positioning, but with the episode of capture or the beginning of their professional service. Catherine Exley rather decided to frame her memoir from birth to death, like another woman, Frances Sophia Rainsford, who experienced captivity through her father, also a redcoat.[57] For both of these women, what was at stake in their writings was a long-term deprivation of 'a certain home', to take up Catherine Exley's words, which they both linked back to their childhood and the loss of their mothers.[58] For them, captivity equated bereavement; and their retrospective life-writing in the mid-nineteenth century served to re-compose a Self dispersed by the enduring impact of war. Ultimately, her text unfolds the story of not merely a prisoner's wife, but a multifaceted female identity in formation as an army wife, a Yorkshire figure, a Methodist convert, amongst other untold Selves, which makes the diary a rare and precious document.

Conclusion

Catherine Elxey's diary unveils the fate of not one but two 'missing spouses', for it is the story of both a husband wrongly given up for dead and sent away to France, and that of a wife, whose narrative illuminates the flagrant absence of research conducted on the prisoners' female companions during the period.[59] Her diary is a rare document, as few female narratives of such Napoleonic experiences have been uncovered so far. It is equally precious, because not only does it provide an insight into Catherine Exley's mind-set, but, more broadly, it also opens up new avenues for a socio-cultural approach to military history, both on a local and transnational scale. It offers an opportunity to further explore early modern experiences of captivity, the shaping of female and religious subjectivities in wartime, along with the civilian and gendered soldiering during the Napoleonic Wars, amongst other expanding fields of historical investigations. Furthermore, if both Frances

Sophia Rainsford's and Catherine Exley's memoirs were recently rediscovered by their descendants, other diaries penned by female actors might be kept in family collections. Once uncovered and rendered public, they could deepen this chapter's brief analytical sketch. Indeed, if numerous questions remain unanswered—authorial intentions can never be fully retrieved, nor considered as an entirely voluntary act—it is perhaps the role of the reader to produce meaning and significance, which allows further interpretations of Catherine Exley's text and future appreciation of the lives and writings of Napoleonic women, whose voices are still seldom heard.[60]

Notes

Abbreviations

ADC   *Archives Départementales de la Creuse*, Guéret

ADG   *Archives Départementales de la Gironde*, Bordeaux

ADM   *Archives Départementales de la Meuse*, Bar-le-Duc

AMV   *Archives Municipales de Verdun*, Verdun

AN   *Archives Nationales*, Paris

SoG   Society of Genealogists, London

(Surnames refer to the works in the *Bibliography* on p.150)

1   *Diary*, p.46.

2   Bell, DA.

3   The expression is inspired by the work of Heather Henderson: see Henderson, p.13.

4   *Diary*, p.46.

5   'Forced journey' is borrowed from Blayney. Lists of British POWs in France are available in: The National Maritime Museum (PRN/6), The National Archives, Kew (ADM 103/441, 468, 486), *Service Historique de la Défense* in Vincennes (YJ 34-81), and Walker pp.312-41. Other French sources on Napoleon's British captives are available in the *Archives Départementales* of each *depots* (9R2 collections),

and the *AN* (F7 collections). Other documents in the *ADG* (e.g. the hospital records at AD 2R212) might provide further information on prisoners in Bordeaux in 1814. The *Bibliography* includes a number of primary sources by prisoners.

6   Garrett, R, p.67.

7   The number is approximate. For a quantitative analysis, see Audin. The British appeared as 'first-class prisoners', especially in comparison to Spanish POWs, who were treated in a far less clement way and served as a labour force: see Aymes, also Lewis, p. 56.

8   In May 1803, Malta became a *casus belli* and Bonaparte ordered the arrest of British civilians on French soil. Hundreds of aristocratic tourists and tradesmen accompanied by their families were declared *'détenus'* (civil hostages) and sent to local depots and thence to Verdun. Legitimized as an extension of the laws of the sea, their arrest was supposed to prevent British men from taking up arms against France. The status of *détenu* (regarded as illegal by the British) was hotly debated, and the word entered the English language; see Chevalley.

9   Approximately 130,000 French were held captive in Britain during the Napoleonic Wars: see Daly, and Le Caravèse.

10 From May of 1793, French law forbade the ransoming of POWs. On the impact of the Enlightenment and the 1789 Revolution on the treatment of POWs, see Crimmin, Jouannet, Hunter, McKibbin, Morieux, and Vourkoutiotis.

11 Brown, G; Morieux, pp.58-62.

12 *ADM* (9R/2); *AMV* (uncatalogued box, *'Les Anglais à Verdun (1803-1814)'*); *AN* (F/7/3310-13, F/7/6337/7101-7107, F/7/6461/9905-9910).

13 For salient studies on Napoleonic experiences of captivity, and differences of treatment in French depots, see Daly, Lewis, Lloyd, and Markham.

14 Birmingham City Archives, Matthew Boulton Papers (MS/37/82/19/1-2).

15 *ADC* (5 Bib 115). Other misspellings, e.g. 'Roncosvalles' for Roncevaux (Fr) or Roncesvalles (Sp), further suggest a language issue.

16 Fraser, E, p.304; census of Guéret's population is online at cassini.ehess.fr.

17 Derainne *et al*, p.140.

18 *Diary*, p.51.

19 Langton, vol.2 p.40.

20 *Diary*, p.46.

21 Blayney, vol.2 p.401.

22 *Diary*, p.47.

23 Fraser, E, p.305.

24 Blayney, vol.2 p.417.

25 *Diary*, p.47.

26 Hain, p.139.

27 *Diary*, p.47.

28 *ADM, Etat civil de Verdun* (2E558(50-60)); SoG (FRA/R6/73007) Wolfe, R, 'Register of births'.

29 Garland McLellan, pp.18-9.

30 *Diary*, p.24.

31 Théofilakis, p.203.

32 Propelled by a feminist school in POW studies, cultural scholars of military history have lately endeavoured to resituate the place of women in captivity, particularly with regards to charity, the construction of the familial space and its regulation by the State: see Biess, Dekel *et al*, Fishman, Hately-Broad, and 'Women: Their absence and their presence' in Lloyd, vol.1 pp.188-95.

33 Aprile.

34 *ADM* (9R2) *'Etat nominatif'* (*10 Nivôse an XII*).

35 Hauterive d', E, vol.1 p.306.

36 Langholm Digital Archives, Hyslop Papers, Letter from James Hyslop to his brother Simon, Verdun (10/10/1804).

37 Chalus and Barker, quoted in Gleadle and Richardson, p.10; Lawrence, vol.1 pp.95, 248.

38 *'Le séjour des femmes anglaises à Verdun'* AMV (uncatalogued box, *'Lettre au sous-préfet'* 11/10/1811).

39 Letter from J. Hyslop (n.36 above).

40 *AN* (F76512); Alger p.282.

41 Hauterive, vol.5 p.81.

42 Regarding the complexity of women's domestic lives during the period, see further Vickery on genteel women in Lancashire.

43 Royal Institute of Cornwall, Courtney Library (uncatalogued) *The Wesleyans of Megavissey* (undated), courtesy of Dr Helen Doe (University of Exeter).

44 'As I drew near the village… written by my husband' *Diary*, p.46. The idea of families as 'communities of intelligence' has been developed with regard to C18th French sailors by Cabantous.

45 Reynolds, quoted in Gleadle and Richardson, p.10.

46 *The Wesleyans of Megavissey* (n.43 above).

47 *Diary*, p.51.

48 Whilst the experience of war was a turning point in Catherine's life, the development of her faith proved equally crucial in shaping her Self, especially as the *Diary* was written after her conversion. In this respect, what appears striking is the entanglement of three levels of time in her writing: that of her experiences, of her narration, and of the *Diary*'s publication.

49 *Diary*, p.58.

50 The recognition of a specific historical consciousness shaping the 'modern Self' was made in the late C18th, especially through Goethe's conceptualisation of Self-formation as the result of 'the interplay of the Self and the world around the Self'. As Steedman argues (*Past Tenses*), this acknowledged historical consciousness provided the 'framework for the emergence of the autobiographical

form', leading to the emergence of the 'memoir' as a genre in Britain around 1800. Zanone went further by arguing that the 1789 Revolution and consecutive wars led to the emergence of a fascination for the 'ego' forged through 'History'. Indeed, sustained by an editorial boom in the aftermath of Waterloo, creating an avid audience through subscriptions on both sides of the Channel, a plethora of memoirs written by civil and military witnesses of the late 'Great War', as they called it, were published: see Esdaile, Lukacs, Porter, and Wahrman.

51 Lejeune.

52 Stendhal.

53 'Next morning we began… was taken prisoner' *Diary*, p.38.

54 The orientation of autobiography from genre studies to their functionality was developed in three seminal works: Bruss, Cadman, and Lynch.

55 Henderson, pp.3-15.

56 We can assume that in the years following their reunion Catherine learnt from Joshua a great deal about life in captivity, and that she would have been able, if she had so wished, to include these details.

57 Garland McLellan.

58 'I had no certain home… counsel me' *Diary*, p.24. On the significance of the mother's death in autobiography, particularly with regard to the theoretical framework developed by Barthes and Derrida on the 'mournful accounts of the mother's dying [as] a way of preserving her body within the body of writing', see Anderson p.113. The motif of the loss of 'home' is also entrenched in a C19th culture of novel writing, which Moretti identifies.

59 *Diary*, p.40.

60 On the importance of the reader, see Barthes, pp.42-8. On the question of the involuntary act of life-writing, see Steedman's '*Enforced Narratives*'.

Sisters in Suffering

comparing French & British women in the Peninsular War

Dr. Thomas Cardoza, Honors Faculty Fellow,
Barrett, The Honors College,
Arizona State University

THOUGH THIS volume is about the war experience of a British woman, women were present in all the armies in the peninsula. France, in particular, had women known as *cantinières* who travelled with each regiment and who shared in its hardships, victories, and defeats. There are many sources for their history, but none of them left as detailed and complete a record as Catherine Exley did. Her memoir, while unique in its own right, tells us a familiar tale of woe and heroism: danger, privation, physical hardship, the loss of loved ones, and, of course, the terrible and unremitting punishment that the weather inflicts on those forced to live outdoors with little shelter and no settled abode.

The nature of women's service with the French Army under Napoleon, while similar, offers a crucial difference from those with the British Army: French women serving as regimental sutlers, or *cantinières*, were more officially integrated into their units than British 'wives on the strength.' British wives accompanying their husbands in the peninsula were more numerous than the officially authorized French *cantinières*, but the French army fully expected all *cantinières* to accompany their units on campaign, where they generally played an active role on the battlefield as a matter of routine, unlike British wives, who faced the likely prospect of being left behind when their husbands shipped out. French *cantinières* were closely integrated into their regiments, even if the War Ministry refused to recognize them as soldiers. They generally saw themselves as soldiers, and their units generally treated them as *militaires* and not as mere camp-followers.

Each *cantinière* held a *patente* or license from her regiment's council of administration, authorizing her to travel with the regiment, and, after 1793, she held this in her own name, not in her husband's. In theory, she had to be married to a soldier in the regiment and be of good moral standing. In practice, during the Empire, the army rarely worried about such niceties. *Cantinières* provided sustenance to the men of their regiments and, since these women received no army pay, supported themselves by selling food and drink, especially alcohol, at a profit. They also acted as laundresses, transporters, moneylenders, nurses, and ran a *cantine* that served as a social centre for the soldiers and officers, since it was one of the few tents in a regiment. As we see continually in Catherine's narrative, shelter was a scarce and precious commodity in an army on the move, and it literally made the difference between life and death.

Already, we can see several key differences between *cantinières* and British wives like Catherine Exley. Catherine had to struggle even to get passage to Portugal, since wives who had or were expecting children were left behind. In the French army, pregnant women went to war and gave birth on campaign, while children also accompanied their parents: the girls as mother's helpers and *cantinières* in training, the boys as officially enrolled *enfants de troupe*, earning uniforms, half pay, and rations starting at age two. So, we could call the French army more family friendly than the British army, though whether sending entire families on campaign was a kindness is highly debatable. Part of this was simple geography: the British forces were clearly fighting an overseas war, and travel by ship for weeks or even months was necessary to get to the theatre of war. As Catherine recounts, this trip might take months and still result in a failure to arrive. On the other hand, the distance between France and Spain could be as short as the span of the bridge at Hendaye over the Bidasoa River. French troops had only to march to Spain, even if that march was arduous. Therefore, there was a physical barrier that mitigated against British wives and families traveling to the peninsula. There was also a psychological barrier: sending women and children involved putting them deliberately on vessels and quite literally shipping them off across the ocean, while for the French, it involved merely marching south. In other words, for the British army, sending wives on campaign was a deliberate and conscious act, while for the French it simply involved carrying on with daily routine.

In addition, the French view of army wives, while similar, was more expansive than the British view. Like British wives, French wives were expected to be useful to the army. Unlike British wives, French *cantinières* had an officially sanctioned position that carried formal duties, and *cantinières* were largely self-sufficient on campaign, gathering plunder or making purchases and reselling the resulting merchandise to the troops at a profit. Therefore, while Catherine's tale is one of almost continual hunger and privation, *cantinières* ate fairly well, had a steady supply of drink, and their husbands and children were consequently better fed and more likely to survive. When Catherine bought bread from a Spaniard at Salamanca for five shillings—a steep price—she could have resold it to an officer for 'a large sum of money,' yet she refused, saying that 'gold was no use to us in our present circumstances.' This echoes a French veteran's statement about *cantinières*' prices: 'That cost a bit sometimes, but money is only good for procuring necessities. The moment one cannot exchange it for bread, gold is worth no more than iron.'[1] It also highlights a difference between her and *cantinières*; Catherine was in desperate need of bread, but in no position to resell it at a profit. She was, in essence, a consumer. *Cantinières*, on the other hand, had the capital, storage, and transport to keep what they needed and resell the rest, providing the officer with his bread and them with a very substantial profit. This was both an excellent survival advantage for the *cantinière* and an important service to the troops. As Boniface de Castellane remarked about life in Spain, 'in an active campaign the lack of sleep means that one needs to replenish one's strength by eating even more: when there is no means to satisfy one's hunger, that is terrible.'[2] Likewise, Captain Montigny commented on the sufferings of soldiers on the march: 'And then you have thirst…. It is suffering if you don't satisfy it and suffering if you succumb to the temptation to quench it: the water is too hot, or too cold, and always unhealthy.' Thus, while alcoholic drinks might seem a quaint luxury, they provided a relatively safe way to quench one's thirst on the march, in camp, or on the battlefield, saving soldiers from dysentery, cholera, and other diseases they could contract from drinking the muddy, polluted water along the way. Likewise, speaking of a miserable night in the rain, he wrote that 'you have to spend a night like that to appreciate the inestimable true value of a simple glass of brandy.'[3]

In a climate like Spain's, *cantinières'* drinks were literally priceless.

Nonetheless, much of the daily life of these women was similar, and when looking at the bigger picture of their sufferings during the war it is important not to overemphasize their differences. Regardless of nationality, marches were pure misery, as Catherine showed when she spoke of walking 'above the knees in mire and wet,' and of sand getting into her clothes, so that it rubbed against her body, causing 'acute pain in walking.' Conditions like these opened the door to exhaustion, illness, and infection. Indeed, the mud in Spain could be more deadly than the enemy, exhausting soldiers and women alike. Boniface de Castellane saw one chasseur à cheval in Spain 'sink into the mud, him and his horse.' Near Valderas, he saw a fusilier kill himself rather than continue through the waist-deep mud.[4] On the other side, Rifleman Harris witnessed men and women who simply gave up and sank to the side of the road to die, their physical and mental powers exhausted by lack of sleep, shelter, and especially food and drink.[5] In these circumstances, Captain Blaze's praise of *cantinières* makes sense:

> These women, endowed with an uncommon energy, were indefatigable; braving heat, cold, rain and snow like old grenadiers, they went out in all directions to procure the items necessary for their commerce. Society people who have never lacked the things necessary for life can't understand how important a bottle of wine or a glass of brandy can be in certain moments.[6]

Most *cantinières* had vehicles, and riding a cart on a muddy road in the rain was less physically exhausting than walking, but carts became stuck and had to be pushed;

they washed away while fording rivers; and they were lost to enemy action, especially when a *cantinière* was captured. French *cantinière* Catherine Campagne lost everything, including her wagon, twice when she was captured. Both times she escaped to make her way back to her unit on foot, in rags, to restart the laborious process of building up her resources from nothing.[7] Another *cantinière* escaped from the prison hulk Argonaut in Cadiz harbour and 'got ashore with little more than a few rags of clothing,' losing her husband to a cannon ball in the process.[8] For such women, life in Spain had few advantages over Catherine Exley's, except that they could look forward to a brighter future through their officially sanctioned commerce.

Laundry was another part of daily life that *cantinières* shared with their British sisters, yet even the status of the humble laundress was complex and ambiguous in Napoleon's armies. The 1793 law authorizing camp-followers provided for two categories of women: *vivandières* (sutlers) and *blanchisseuses* (laundresses), allowing up to four *blanchisseuses* per battalion, and as many *vivandières* as the commander deemed necessary. The open-ended number of *vivandières* was the subject of much abuse, and under Napoleon a new law of 1800 limited the total number of women per battalion to four, regardless of their nominal function.[9] By the time of the Peninsular War, these distinctions had broken down and become irrelevant to the men and women at the front. Few French soldiers referred to sutlers as *'vivandières'* by 1808, and few French camp-followers were officially *'blanchisseuses'*. Rather, front line soldiers referred to their sutlers by the more modern term *'cantinières'*, and the *cantinière* acted as both sutler and laundress. British wives certainly did laundry, and while they did not have official sanction to operate as sutlers to the entire regiment, they cooked and at times procured food for their husbands, built campfires, and in general shared with their French sisters the drudgery of housekeeping on campaign.

Like much of their daily lives in the field, the origins of French army women show strong similarities with Catherine Exley's. Despite her assertion that her mother was 'rich', Catherine was of working-class origins, like almost all of her French counterparts. Her early life trajectory was typical for a young French *cantinière*, or for most young women who followed a military career, including those who enlisted as men.[10] The daughter of a working-class father, Catherine was orphaned at twelve and hired herself out as a domestic servant at age nineteen: these circumstances were all typical of the young women who travelled with the Napoleonic armies. Likewise, while living alone and working in a dead-end occupation, she met a soldier, fell in love, and, with no real ties to bind her to civilian life, began following the drum. As Catherine put it: 'I had no certain home, no parents, no kind friends with whom I could advise.' For poverty-stricken, desperate, and rootless young women, marrying a soldier offered a glimmer of hope for a new life, even if that life turned out to be harsh and often short. Many young French women faced similar situations. Domestic servants living away from home were an important component of the French *cantinière* corps, undoubtedly because of the very same conditions that compelled Catherine to marry a soldier and follow him to war: lack of local family ties was crucial. Living alone, often in a strange town, young serving women across Europe found it easier to meet young soldiers than if they were living under their parents' roofs.[11] Jeanne Demonay was a servant living away from home when she met and married a soldier of the 15th Infantry regiment.[12] Likewise, young French women without parents were, like Catherine, prime candidates for a military life. Marie Elisabeth Peter was an orphan from Alsace who ended up marrying a cavalryman, while Marie Pierrette, a foundling from Provence, married an infantryman.[13] For both, it was a step up.

Finally, we need to discuss the hereditary *cantinière*, born and raised in the army. While hardly a majority, these women represented a substantial number of French camp-followers, and they tended to stay in service long-term, despite the loss of husbands. Catherine Campagne was one such woman. Born twelve years before Catherine Exley in 1767 to a soldier of the Royal Army and his *vivandière* wife, Campagne grew up in the army and became a *vivandière* herself in 1783, at age sixteen. She served in this capacity for thirty-one years, spending several years in Spain. Twice captured and imprisoned, she lost her wagon and everything she owned on both occasions. Both times, she escaped and returned to the French army, then built up her fortune again. Two of her husbands were killed in the fighting around Saragossa in 1812. Campagne served until 1814, finally begging for a pension in 1815 when she went home with no money or income.[14]

This brings us to a final and regrettable point, one that most war stories leave out entirely: the many years of civilian drudgery and poverty that faced these women once the wars ended in 1814-15. While war narratives quite understandably focus on the events of the war years, what happened to the millions of veterans and the tens of thousands of women camp-followers after the war is arguably more important to our understanding of nineteenth-century Europe than their exploits during the actual wars, and in most cases they are sad stories indeed. Catherine and Joshua Exley eked out a precarious existence after his discharge, and this was also common among *cantinières*. Like Catherine, *cantinières* faced poverty in their old age. There were many plaintive petitions to the War Ministry in the years 1815-20 from desperate former *cantinières* and *blanchisseuses* begging for a pension or even placement in the Royal Army as a way to earn their bread. All too often, the restored monarchy denied these claims, leaving the women in misery.[15] Some *cantinières* did prosper for a while in Spain, and even made small fortunes. Sylvain Larreguy de Civrieux was a wealthy cadet when he arrived in Spain in 1813. He wrote: 'the *vivandières* vied with each other to entice me; I became the soul of their *cantines*, and men swore by me in their open air cabarets.' After fifteen days of this treatment, the rich young man was penniless.[16] This lends credence to the story relayed by Professor Esdaile of 'a young woman who had marched into Spain in 1808 with nothing more than a cask of brandy on her hip, but by 1812 was riding in a grand carriage and dressed in the finest clothes.'[17] Yet one wonders what happened to this young entrepreneur in the following two years. Did she make her escape to France with all her loot, or did she lose everything as Catherine Campagne did? Was she killed, as many *cantinières* were? Or did she end up like Mme. Fetter, a *cantinière* who, at age 93 in 1880, was still living in utter poverty in the aptly named Rue des Martyrs in Paris, nursing a widow's pension granted in 1829, which was rendered utterly insignificant by inflation?[18] We do not know, but clearly many French *cantinières*, however much they may have profited in wartime, ended the wars in poverty, and in many cases were refused pensions too.

Cathcrine's experience in her old age is similar to many *cantinières*, with the notable exception that Catherine learned to write so she could record her story for posterity. That shows a larger sense of purpose and a deeper understanding of her own historical significance than the French *cantinières* appear to have had, and it makes her story even more remarkable. Sadly, no such comprehensive memoirs have come to us from French *cantinières*, leaving us to sift through scraps of evidence to get a picture of their lives. For that reason, we should all be grateful to Catherine. Her story is familiar, but it adds richness, depth, and colour to our understanding of women in the Peninsular War. It also helps confirm many of our previous discoveries and beliefs, and, for a historian, that sort of validation is as priceless as a glass of brandy after a cold night in the rain.

Notes

(Surnames refer to the works in the *Bibliography* on p.150)

1   Blaze, E, p.49.

2   Castellane, I:148.

3   Montigny, pp.67, 79-80.

4   Castellane, I:48, I:41.

5   Harris, pp.82-83, 101.

6   Blaze, E, p.49.

7   *'Sabatier, née Campagne'* Xs12, *Service Historique des Armées, Armée de Terre (AT).*

8   Elting, p.613.

9   *'Arrêté relatif aux enfants de troupe, et aux femmes à la suite de l'armée,' Journal Militaire,* 2ème *Semestre,* An 8, 751.

10 See Steinberg.

11 See the memoirs of numerous soldiers, especially Chevillet.

12 *'Gerard, née Démonay'* Xs11, *AT.*

13 *'Bory, née Peter'* Xs11, *AT; 'Hoccard, née Pierrette'* Xs12, *AT.*

14 *'Sabatier, née Campagne'* (see n.7)

15 See for example in *AT 'Archevêque', 'Sabatier, née Campagne'* and *'Billers, née Pauli'.*

16 Larreguy de Civrieux, pp.90-1.

17   Esdaile.

18   'A *Cantinière* of the First Empire' in *New York Times*, 27
     April 1880.

Women in the Peninsular War

Prof. Charles Esdaile, University of Liverpool

IT IS A curious fact, but, setting aside a handful of senior commanders, the most famous combatant of the Peninsular War is a woman. I refer, of course, to Agustina Zaragoza Domenech, a young Catalan girl who on 2 July 1808, beat off a French attack on Zaragoza singlehanded by manning a cannon whose crew had all just been cut down by a shell.[1] This story is an important one as it gave rise to one of the two dominant images that we have of the women of Spain and Portugal in the Peninsular War. Thus Agustina is the patriotic heroine *par excellence*, the woman who rushes to the barricades to defend hearth and home and king and country and through her sheer frailty encourages the men around her to regain their courage and fight that much harder, while the fact that Goya immortalised her great feat of arms in the famous 'Disasters of War' ensured that its memory would become absorbed by an interna- tional audience rather than just a Spanish one—in the engraving entitled *'Que valor!'* ('What courage!'), we see the slim figure of Agustina not just standing erect and defiant beside an enormous fieldpiece, but also symboli- cally shielding the observer from an unseen opponent. Nor, meanwhile, is this the only engraving in the series that projects the idea of the woman as combatant, albeit perhaps as a temporary one who takes up arms only in dire emergency. Thus, in *'Y son fieras'* ('And they, too, are furies') a group of women who have obviously been taken by surprise by a party of French troops—one of them is carrying a baby under her arm—are seen fighting desperately to defend themselves with a variety of improvised weapons. Less dramatic, but otherwise rather similar is *'Las mujeres dan valor'* ('The women inspire courage') in which we see two women locked in combat with two French soldiers who have evidently been trying to rape them, and *'No quieren'* ('They don't love') in which a French soldier grapples with a girl while an old woman—possibly her mother, perhaps—steals up behind him with a knife poised to stab him in the back. However, striking though these four engravings are—engravings which, it should be stressed, in no way imply that women were anything other than occasional combatants—on looking at the 'Disasters of War' as a whole, we generally see women rather as the helpless victims of man's inhumanity. In *'Tampoco'* ('Nor this'), *'Ni por esas'* ('Not even for these'), *'Amarga presencia'* ('Bitter presence'), *'Ya no hay tiempo'* ('There is no longer any time'), women are seen being raped; in *'No se puede mirar'* ('One cannot look') they figure in a mass execution; in *'Estragos de la guerra'* ('War damage'), they are crushed in the wreckage of a collapsing building; in *'Escapan de las llamas'* ('Escaping from the flames'), *'Yo lo vi'* ('I saw this') and *'Y esto también'* ('And this too'), they become fugitives and refugees; in *'Que alboroto es este?'* ('What is all this row'?), they collapse in floods of tears on receiving bad news, possibly, given the context, of the death or execution of a son or husband; and, finally in *'Cruel lástima'* ('Cruel misfortune'), *'Caridad de una mujer'* ('Charity of a woman'), *'Madre infeliz'* ('Unhappy mother'), *'Gracias a la almorta'* ('Thanks be to vetch'), *'No llegan a tiempo'* ('They did not arrive in time'), *'Sanos y enfermos'* ('Healthy and sick'), *'De que sirve una taza?'* ('What is the use of a cup?') and *'Si son de otro linaje'* ('If they are of other lineage'), they are seen begging in the streets or succumbing to famine and disease.[2]

In 'The Disasters of War', then, women are either heroines or victims, or, indeed, sometimes both at once. Before going any further, however, let us first admit that, to a greater or lesser extent, evidence can be found to support most aspects of the heroine/victim syndrome. Beginning first of all with the idea of women as combatants, Agustina Zaragoza is not the only example that we can find of women who took up arms against the French, there being both British and French accounts of women fighting with guerrilla bands.[3] At the same time it is at least possible that, impelled by the murder of her father and brother in the French occupation of Bilbao in August of 1808, a young Basque woman named María Martina Ibaibarriaga for a time actually headed a guerrilla band in the Cantabrian mountains and eventually gained a commission in the Spanish army, although it is important to note that she did so disguised as a man, while there are also references to women taking part in skirmishes in the Serranía de Ronda.[4] Finally, here and there are to be found tales of heroines in the style of Agustina de Aragón: in La Palma de Condado (Huelva), for example, according to local tradition, a tavern keeper named María Marcos played a key role in driving out a small force of French troops that was attacked in the town on 9 March 1811.[5] A variant on the theme, here, is the issue of the murder of isolated French soldiers. Travelling to Madrid after the battle of Bailén, for example, the British liaison officer, Samuel Whittingham, was introduced to a peasant woman who was supposed to have killed eight French soldiers by knocking them on the head as they were drinking from her well and then throwing them down its shaft.[6] This case can be dismissed as mere patriotic nonsense, but it is nonetheless interesting that a woman could have persuaded the local community to accept such a claim (and still more interesting that she should have been moved to make it), whilst from time to time rumours also surfaced amongst the French that Spanish women were taking unwary soldiers to their beds so as later to do away with them.[7]

If some women fought, meanwhile, others became fierce advocates of the Patriot cause and thereby broke the bounds of the very narrow frame in which the vast majority of Spanish and Portuguese women tended to be constrained. Stationed at Chiclana during the siege of Cádiz, for example, a military pharmacist attached to the corps of Marshal Victor named Antoine Fée, who was billeted in the home of a prominent local citizen named Múñoz, found himself constantly assailed by one of the household's three daughters, a fiery young woman named María who 'took hatred of the French to a state of exultation'.[8] Meanwhile, still another way for women actively to involve themselves in the patriotic struggle was to become a spy, one such case that has been uncovered being that of María García, a housewife from Ronda who took it upon herself to pass information of all kinds to the local partisans, and two others those of María Isidora de Gastañaga and Manuela Rubín López, both of whom were sentenced to terms of imprisonment for espionage in the Basque provinces.[9] And, finally, there was also always the possibility of engaging in acts of symbolic resistance—the French hussar, Albert de Rocca, saw Andalusian women wearing 'English stuffs on which the pictures of Ferdinand VII and the Spanish generals most distinguished in the war against the French were painted'[10]—or, alternatively, solidarity with the Allied cause: when the governor of Seville invited 200 of the leading ladies of the city to a ball celebrating Joseph's saint's day on 19 March 1810, the only ones who turned up were forty who were 'so dishonest that they were the scandal of the crowd that out of mere curiosity had gathered to inspect the decorations that had been put up to mark the occasion', whilst here one may also cite a number of incidents mentioned in British memoirs in which local girls succoured officers who had been taken prisoner by the French or otherwise fallen upon hard times.[11]

As involvement in the struggle was naturally accompanied by suffering in the struggle—sadly, the female experience of the Peninsular War was often one of great misery—there is clearly no smoke without fire, but this is but the beginning of the story. The first and most obvious thing to say here, perhaps, is that, as the rival armies tramped to and fro across the Iberian Peninsula, they attracted large numbers of women to their ranks. As early as the autumn of 1808 there were complaints about the crowds of camp followers hanging around the Spanish forces, and it was not long before the French and Anglo-Portuguese forces began to experience the same phenomenon.[12] Some of those who took to following the drum were the wives of men who had enlisted or been conscripted or killed and had no other means of support, while others were professional prostitutes, but still others 'kept the camp fires burning' for reasons that were more complex. First of all, there were women who genuinely fell in love with French or British officers and took to the road with them, the best example here being Juana de León, a young girl rescued from the sack of Badajoz, who married a Lieutenant Harry Smith and was eventually, as Lady Smith, commemorated by the town of that name in South Africa.[13] And, second of all, there were plenty of women who entered the world of the military for reasons of calculation, whether it was simply to escape starvation or save themselves from molestation at the hands of the guerrillas or marauding troops, or because it offered a chance to break away from home lives that were at best stultifying and at worst little better than chattel slavery (not, of course, that these factors excluded the possibility of falling in love: indeed, in some instances they may even have increased the likelihood of doing so). Except in a handful of cases—an example might be 'a beautiful Spanish girl' who supposedly became the 'house-keeper' of the governor of Andujar so as 'to escape the brutality of the brigands'[14]—why individual women acted as they did, we shall never know, but what we can be certain of is that by the end of the war literally thousands of women had left their homes in favour of a life of camps and campaigns: hence the 'oceans of women' whom happy British soldiers remembered capturing at Vitoria.[15]

Not all women who took up with the invaders necessarily went to war. On the contrary, many relationships were evidently rather conducted wholly in the context of garrison life or, more fleetingly, the brief encounters that were the inevitable result of large numbers of troops who were constantly on the move from one battlefield to the next. Of such love affairs, both sides' memoirs are full—good examples include those of Charles Parquin, Nicolas Marcel and Augustus Schaumann[16]—and, assuming that they are something other than fantasy pure and simple, attempts to obscure a darker reality or encounters with prostitutes clever enough to hide the reality of the work in which they were engaged, it is not impossible that these, too, contained an element of rebellion or sexual adventure; indeed, here and there we come across references to women who seem quite literally to have been 'party animals' bent on nothing more than making hay while the sun shone.[17]

A point that is particularly interesting to speculate upon here is the extent to which the activities, amatory or otherwise, that women engaged in were symptomatic of a degree of political engagement with the struggle, even, indeed, of a degree of political awareness. This, however, is an issue that is problematic in the extreme. Modern-day Spanish feminists are very anxious to claim that the women of 1808-14 were just as patriotic as their male counterparts were, and therefore to see every act of what appears to be engagement with the struggle as evidence of the patriotism that they are desperate to find, but the fact is that, except in the case of a few élite women—the Condesa de Bureba, Frasquita Larrea, the Marquesa de Villafranca—who became heavily involved in the Patriot cause, the picture that we have is at best one of ambiguity. In *Napoleon's Cursed War*, for example, Ronald Fraser—a writer who, if not a feminist, is at all times anxious to portray the Spanish struggle as a veritable 'people's war'—has produced some 268 cases of women who were tried by the *afrancesado* authorities for what he claims to have been involvement in *la guerrilla*, but, when deconstructed, these crimes—for example, receiving stolen goods—appear just as likely to have been committed in the context of brigandage as in that of fighting the French.[18] The same problems present themselves in respect of the response of Spanish women to moments of liberation at the hands of British troops. For example, many British memoirists paint a dramatic picture of the joyful scenes that occurred when Wellington's army entered Madrid on August 12th, 1812. However, were the women who mobbed the redcoats seeking custom, welcoming liberation from the French, expressing sexual excitement, or simply celebrating the end of many months of misery and famine?[19]

Meanwhile, much the same is true of women who elected to follow the French. From time to time veterans of the conflict can be found arguing that they were moved by sympathy for the French, or, at least, that, having fled to the French in an attempt to flee cottage or convent, they became 'ardent francophiles'.[20] Well, perhaps, but only in one instance—that of a secularised nun who denounced a parish priest for spreading pro-Patriot rumours[21]—has an incident been uncovered that could possibly be explained in terms of ideological conviction, while the fact that women who were captured by the Anglo-Portuguese forces at Vitoria and other actions quickly found new protectors rather suggests that sympathy for French ideas was not an issue. As one British officer put it, 'As long as women [can] dance, I believe they don't much care with whom.'[22] Occasionally, true, one does find rueful references to the French making far more conquests in Spain than the British did, but even if this could be proved to be the case, it can easily be explained by reference to the fact that the French presence tended to be much more permanent that did that of Wellington's army, and all the more so as the latter seems to have done just as well as the French in Portugal.[23]

In the end, then, one has to say that the Peninsular War brought little change for the women of Spain and Portugal. Whilst this offered a certain number a chance to escape from their immediate surroundings, the choice that they made was at best a risky one, and one that often involved them in further servitude. Nor in many instances were they even allowed to pursue their new roles for good. Many of the Spanish and Portuguese women who joined the French army as wives or lovers may be assumed to have followed their soldier-partners to France when they retreated across the frontier, but in the British army the situation was very different, the only women allowed to travel with Wellington's army when it embarked for home in August of 1814 being those who could prove that they were legally married. All the others being forcibly cast off and marched back to the Pyrenees in the custody of a column of Portuguese troops, following the drum did not in the end prove much of an option, the most that can be said for it being that it had provided some thousands of women with a means of keeping body and soul together in the midst of a time of near total economic and social collapse. Yet women were not just victims of the conflict. Rather, they had also been participants in it, and in this fashion 'became visible' in a fashion that had never been the case before. As a step on the road to women's liberation it was a small one indeed, but it was nonetheless one that had to be taken.

Notes

(Surnames refer to the works in the *Bibliography* on p.150)

1 For the story of Agustina Zaragoza, see Tone.

2 For a convenient gateway to *'Los desastres de la guerra'*, see gasl.org/refbib/Goya__Guerra.pdf.

3 Malmesbury, vol.2, pp.258-9; Butler, vol.2 p.271.

4 Sánchez Arresiegor, in Miranda, vol.1, pp.709-13; Haythornthwaite, pp.134-5.

5 Cf. scribd.com/doc/27464846/La-Palma-Del-Condado.

6 Whittingham, pp.39-40.

7 E.g. Thirion, pp.87-91.

8 Fée, p.66.

9 Reder Gadow, M; *Gazeta de Oficio del Gobierno de Vizcaya*, 27 April 1810, p.3; sentence of the *Junta Criminal de Alava*, 19 June 1812, *Instituto de Historia y Cultura Militar* (Madrid), *Cuartel General del Ejército del Norte* 7343.229.

10 Haythornthwaite, p.123.

11 Anon., *'Noticias de Sevilla'* (ms.), n.d., *Archivo Histórico Nacional, Sección de Estado, legajo* 2994, No.4. For two cases of feminine generosity towards British officers, cf. Bell, G, p.46, and Oman, pp.185-6.

12 See the proclamation of Francisco Javier Castaños, 27 June 1808, *Archivo de los Condes de Bureta, Papeles de Palafox*; Wylly, pp.32, 91.

13 The history of León can best be followed in Moore-Smith.

14 Blayney, vol.1, p.157.

15 Bell, p.94, also Dallas, vol.3, p.289, and Blaze, vol.2, p.254.

16 See Jones, Var, and Ludovici.

17 That many women had to turn to prostitution to survive is all too obvious: e.g. Ludovici, p.355. Meanwhile, for two women who were evidently bent on having a good war, see Grivel, pp.239-40, and Clemenso, pp.32-3.

18 Fraser, pp.430-1; also Sánchez Arreseigor, pp.704-8.

19 References to this episode are numerous: e.g. Page, p.191, Liddell Hart, p.91, and Grattan, vol.2 pp.II, 90.

20 North, p.87.

21 See Orti Belmonte, pp.148-9.

22 *Cit.* Malmesbury, vol.2 pp.261-2.

23 Cf. Dallas, vol.3 p.294. For a good example of a British officer lamenting the greater success of his French opponents with Spanish women, see Grattan, vol.2 pp.95-6.

Bibliography

Alger, JG. *Englishmen in the French Revolution* (Searle & Rivington, 1889)

Anderson, L. *Autobiography* (Routledge, 2001)

Aprile, S. *'De l'exilé à l'exilée: une histoire sexuée de la proscription politique outre-Manche et outre-Atlantique sous le Second Empire'* (2008) 225:4 *Le Mouvement Social* pp.27-38

Ashbridge, E. *Some Account of the Early Part of the Life of Elizabeth Ashbridge* (1807)

Audin, M. 'British Hostages in Napoleonic France. The Evidence with particular reference to manufacturers and artisans' (University of Birmingham, MA thesis, 1987)

Aymes, JR. *La déportation sous le Premier Empire. Les Espagnols en France (1808-1814)* (Sorbonne, 1983)

Bacon, MH. (ed) *Wilt Thou Go On My Errand? Journals of Three 18th Century Quaker Women Ministers* (Pendle Hill, 1994)

Barthes, R. 'The Death of the Author', in Barthes, *Image-Music-Text*, trans./ed. Heath, S. (Fontana, 1977)

Bell, DA. *The First Total War: Napoleon's Europe and the Birth of Warfare as We Know It* (Houghton Miflin, 2007)

Bell, G. *Rough Notes by an Old Soldier during Fifty Years' Service* (London, 1867 and repr. 1956)

Biess, F. *Homecomings: Returning POWs and the Legacies of Defeat in Postwar Germany* (Princeton, 2006)

Blayney, A. *Narrative of a Forced Journey through France and Spain as a Prisoner of War in the Years 1810 to 1814* (London, 1814)

Blaze, E. *Souvenirs d'un officier de la Grande Armée* (Fayard, undated)

Boys, E. *Narrative of a Captivity, Escape, and Adventures in France and Flanders During the War* (Newby, 1863)

Brown, G. 'Prisoner of War Parole: Ancient Concept, Modern Utility' (1998) 156 *Military Law Review*

Bruss, EW. *Autobiographical Acts: The Changing Situation of a Literary Genre* (Johns Hopkins, 1976)

Burgess, J. 'The Quakers, the Brethren and the Religious Census in Cumbria' (1980) 80 *Transactions of the Cumberland & Westmorland Antiquarian & Archaeological Society* 104

Burnham, R. and McGuigan, R. *The British Army against Napoleon: Facts, Lists and Trivia* (Frontline, 2010)

Butler, AJ. (ed) *The Memoirs of Baron Thiébault, late Lieutenant-General in the French Army* (London, 1896)

Cabantous, A. *Dix mille marins face à l'Océan. Les populations maritimes de Dunkerque au Havre aux XVIIe et XVIIIe siècles (vers 1660-1794). Étude Sociale* (Publisud, 1991)

Cadman, S. *Generating Texts: The Progeny of Seventeenth-Century Prose* (University of Virginia, 1996)

Castellane, B de. *Journal du Maréchal Castellane* (Plon, 1895-97)

Chalus, E. and Barker, H. (eds) *Gender in Eighteenth-century England: Roles, Representations and Responsibilities* (Longman, 1997)

Chevillet, J. *Ma Vie Militaire, 1800-1809* (Hachette, 1906)

Chevalley, E. *Essai sur le Droit des Gens Napoléonien 1800-1807. D'après la correspondance* (Delagrave, undated), vol.1

Chilcote, PW. *John Wesley and the Women Preachers of Early Methodism* (American Theological Library Association and Scarecrow Press, 1991)

Clemenso, H. (ed. Zermastten) *Souvenirs d'un officier valaisan au service de France* (Paris, 1999)

Coss, E. *All for the King's Shilling: the British Soldier under Wellington, 1808-1814* (Oklahoma, 2010)

Crimmin, PK. 'Prisoners of War and British Port Communities, 1793-1815' (1996) 6:4 *The Northern Mariner / Le Marin du Nord* 17-27

Crowley, JE. 'The Sensibility of Comfort' (1999) 104/3 *American Historical Review* 749-782; *The Invention of Comfort: Sensibilities and Design in Early Modern Britain and Early America* (Johns Hopkins, 2001)

Dallas, A. *Félix Alvarez, or Manners in Spain, containing Descriptive Accounts of Some of the Prominent Events of the late Peninsular War and Authentic Anecdotes Illustrative of the Spanish Character* (London, 1818)

Daly, G. 'Napoleon's Lost Legions: French Prisoners of War in Britain, 1803-1814' (2004) 89 *History* 361-80

Dekel, R. *et al* 'Trapped in Captivity: Marital Perceptions of Wives of Former Prisoners of War' (2005) 42:3 *Women Health* 1-18

Dempsey, G. *Albuera, 1811: the Bloodiest Battle of the Peninsular War* (Frontline, 2008)

Derainne *et al* (eds) *Les Etrangers en France: guide des sources d'archives publiques et privées: XIXe-XXe siècles* (Génériques, 2005)

Ellison, S. *Prison Scenes: And Narrative of Escape from France, during the Late War* (Whittaker, 1838)

Elting, J. *Swords Around a Throne: Napoleon's Grande Armée* (Da Capo, 1988)

Esdaile, C. *The Peninsular War: a New History* (Allen Lane, 2002); *Peninsular Eyewitnesses: The Experience of War in Spain and Portugal 1808-1813* (Pen & Sword, 2008); 'Bullets, Baggages and Ballads: Forgotten Sources for the Study of the Experience of British Women in the Peninsular War' in Duarte, MD. (ed) *Da Guerra Peninsular: retratos e representações* (Lisbon, 2011) 13-38

Fée, ALA. *Souvenirs de la Guerre d'Espagne, dite de l'Independence, 1809-1813* (Paris, 1856)

Fishman, S. *We Will Wait: Wives of French Prisoners of War, 1940-1945* (Yale, 1991)

Fletcher, I. *In the Service of the King: the Letters of William Thornton Keep at Home, Walcheren and in the Peninsula, 1808-1814* (Spellmount, 1997)

Forbes, J. *Letters from France, written in the Years 1803 and 1804: Including a Particular Account of Verdun, and the Situation of the British Captives in that City* (White, 1806)

Fraser, E. *Napoleon the Gaoler, Personal Experiences and Adventures of British Sailors and Soldiers during the Great Captivity* (Methuen, 1914)

Fraser, R. *Napoleon's Cursed War: Spanish Popular Resistance in the Peninsular War* (London, 2008)

Frost, JW. *The Quaker Family in Colonial America: A Portrait of the Society of Friends* (St Martin's, 1973)

Reder Gadow, M. '*Espionaje y represión en la Serranía de Ronda: María García, "La Tinajera", un ejemplo de coraje ante los franceses*', in Castells *et al* (eds), *Heroínas y patriotas: mujeres de 1808* (Madrid, 2009) 175-92

Garland McLellan, J. (ed) *Recollections of my Childhood: The True Story of a Childhood lived in the Shadow of Napoleon Bonaparte* (CreateSpace, 2010)

Garrett, R. *P.O.W: The Uncivil Face of War* (David & Charles, 1988)

Gleadle, K. and Richardson, S. *Women in British Politics, 1760-1860. The Power of the Petticoat* (Macmillan, 2000)

Grassby, R. 'Material Culture and Cultural History', (2005) *Journal of Interdisciplinary History* 35/4 591-603

Grattan, W. *Adventures of the Connaught Rangers from 1808 to 1814* (London, 1847)

Grivel, J. *Mémoires du Vice-Amiral Baron Grivel* (Paris, 1914)

Haig, MH. *The History of Batley 1800-1974* (Haig, 1978)

Hain, E. (ed) *Prisoners of War in France from 1804 to 1814, Being the Adventures of John Tregerthen Short and Thomas Williams of Saint-Ives* (Duckworth & Co., 1914)

Harris, B. *The Recollections of Rifleman Harris* (Archon, 1970)

Hately-Broad, B. *War and Welfare: British Prisoner of War Families, 1939-45* (Manchester, 2009)

Hauterive d', E. *La police secrète du Premier Empire, bulletins quotidiens adressés par Fouché à l'Empereur, 1804-1807* (Perrin et Cie, 1908)

Haythornthwaite, P. (ed) *In the Peninsula with a French Hussar* (London, 1990); *Redcoats: the British Soldiers of the Napoleonic Wars* (Pen & Sword, 2012)

Henderson, H. *The Victorian Self. Autobiography, and Biblical Narrative* (Cornell, 1989)

Hewson, M. *Escape from the French, Captain Hewson's Narrative (1803-1809)* (Hodder & Stoughton, 1891)

Hinds, H. *God's Englishwomen: Seventeenth-Century Radical Sectarian Writing and Feminist Criticism* (Manchester, 1996)

Hoffman, F. *A Sailor of King George. The Journals of Captain Frederick Hoffman R.N. 1793-1814* (Murray, 1901)

Hunter, I. 'Kant and Vattel in Context: Cosmopolitan Philosophy and Diplomatic Casuistry' (2013) 39:4 *History of European Ideas* 477-502

Hyslop Booth, D. (ed) *Shepherd, Sailor and Survivor: The Life and Letters of James Hyslop, RN, 1764-1853* (Booth, 2010)

Jones, BT. (ed) *Military Memoirs of Charles Parquin* (London, 1987)

Jouannet, E. *Vattel and the Emergence of Classic International Law* (Hart, 2009)

King, S. *Poverty and Welfare in England 1700-1850: A Regional Perspective* (Manchester, 2000)

Langton, R. *Narrative of a Captivity in France from 1809 to 1814* (Smith, 1836)

Larreguy de Civrieux, S. *Souvenirs d'un cadet, 1812-1823* (Hachette, 1912)

Lawrence, J. *A Picture of Verdun, or The English Detained in France* (Hookham, 1810)

Le Caravèse, P. 'Les prisonniers français en Grande-Bretagne de 1803 à 1814' (2010) 3:9 *Napoleonica. La Revue* 118-152

Lejeune, P. *L'autobiographie en France* (Colin, 1971)

Lemire, B. 'Peddling Fashion: Salesmen, Pawnbrokers, Tailors, Thieves and the Second-hand Clothes Trade in England, c. 1700-1800' (1991) *Textile History* 22/1 67-82

Levy, B. *Quakers and the American Family* (OUP, 1988)

Lewis, M. *Napoleon and his British Captives* (Allen & Unwin, 1962)

Liddell Hart, BH. (ed) *The Letters of Private Wheeler* (London, 1951)

Linch, K. *Britain and Wellington's Army: Recruitment, Society and Tradition, 1750-1850* (Houndmills, 2011)

Lloyd, CL. *A History of Napoleonic and American Prisoners of War, 1756-1816: Hulk, Depot and Parole* (Woodbridge, 2007)

Ludovici, A. (ed) *On the Road with Wellington: the Diary of a War Commissary in the Peninsular Campaigns* (New York, 1925)

Lukacs, J. *Historical Consciousness: The Remembered Past* (Harper & Row, 1968)

Lynch, K. *Protestant Autobiography in the Seventeenth-Century Anglophone World* (OUP, 2012)

Malmesbury, Third Earl (ed) *A Series of Letters of the First Earl of Malmesbury, his Family and Friends from 1745 to 1820* (London, 1870)

Markham, D. 'Prisoners and Writers: Napoleon's British Captives and Their Stories' (1996) 26 *Consortium on Revolutionary Europe, 1750-1850* 121-34

Matthews, DA. 'War Wellingtons: Military Footwear in the Age of Empire', in Riello, G. and McNeil, P. (eds) *Shoes: A History from Sandals to Sneakers* (Berg, 2006)

McKibbin, MA. 'Citizens of liberty, agents of tyranny: the dual perception of allied prisoners of war during the French Revolution' (1996) 26 *Consortium on Revolutionary Europe, 1750-1850* 112-120

Miranda, F. *'Guerra, sociedad y política (1808-1814)': Congreso internacional: Pamplona y Tudela, 21-24 de noviembre de 2007*

Montigny, L. *Souvenirs anecdotiques d'un officier de la Grande Armée* (Gosselin, 1833)

Moore-Smith, GC. (ed) *The Autobiography of Sir Harry Smith, 1787-1819* (London, 1910)

Moretti, F. *The Way of the World: The Bildungsroman in European Culture* (London, 1987)

Morieux, R. 'French prisoners of war, conflicts of honour and social inversions in England, 1744-1783' (2013) 56:1 *Historical Journal* 55-88

Noakes, G. *The History of the 34th and 55th Regiments by George Noakes late QMSgt. 55th* (Charles Thurman, 1875)

North, J. (ed) *In the Legions of Napoleon: the Memoirs of a Polish Officer in Spain and Russia, 1808-1813* (London, 1999)

O'Brien, DH. *My Adventures in the Late War: Comprising a Narrative of Shipwreck, Captivity, Escapes from French prisons* (Arnold, 1814)

Oman, C. (ed) 'A prisoner of Albuera: the Journal of Major William Brooke from 16 May to 28 September 1811' in Oman, C. *Studies in the Napoleonic Wars* (Oxford, 1929); *A History of the Peninsular War* (Oxford, 1902-1930)

Orti Belmonte, J. *Córdoba en la Guerra de la Independencía* (Córdoba, 1930)

Page, J. (ed) *Intelligence Officer in the Peninsula: Letters and Diaries of Major the Honourable Charles Somers Cocks, 1786-1812* (Tunbridge Wells, 1986)

Porter, R. *Rewriting the Self. Histories from the Renaissance to the Present* (Routledge, 1997)

Proudfoot Montagu, E. *The Personal Narrative of the Escape of Edward Proudfoot Montagu: An English Prisoner of War, from the Citadel of Verdun* (Beccles, 1849)

Pyne, WH. *'Camp Scenes', Etchings by and after W. H. Pyne* (Pyne and Nattes, 1803)

Raikes, H. (ed) *Memoir of Vice-Admiral Sir Jahleel Brenton, Bart.* (Hatchard, 1846)

Reynolds, KD. *Aristocratic Women and Political Society in Victorian Britain* (Clarendon, 1998)

Riello, G. *Cotton: The Fabric that Made the Modern World* (CUP, 2013); *A Foot in the Past: Consumers, Producers and Footwear in the Long Eighteenth Century* (OUP, 2006)

Sánchez Arreisegor, JJ. *'Mujeres en la guerra'* in Miranda, F. (ed) *Guerra, Sociedad y Política, 1808-1814* (Pamplona, 2008)

Sherer, JM. *Recollections of the Peninsula* (London, 1824)

Steedman, CK. 'Enforced Narratives' in Cosslett (ed) *Feminism and Autobiography. Texts, Theories, Methods* (Routledge, 2000) 25-39; *Past Tenses: Essays on Writing, Autobiography and History* (Rivers Oram, 1992)

Steinberg, S. *La confusion des sexes: La travestissement de la Renaissance à la Révolution* (Fayard, 2001)

Stendhal, *La Chartreuse de Parme* (Hetzel, 1846)

Sturt, C. *The Real State of France in the Year 1809, with an Account of the Treatment of Prisoners of War and Persons Otherwise Detained in France* (Ridgway, 1810)

Styles, J. 'Custom or Consumption? Plebeian Fashion in Eighteenth-Century England', in Berg, M. and Eger, E. (eds) *Luxury in the Eighteenth Century: Debates, Desires and Delectable Goods* (Palgrave, 2003) 103-18; *The Dress of the People: Everyday Fashion in Eighteenth-Century England* (Yale, 2007)

Théofilakis, F. *'La sexualité du prisonnier de guerre'* (2008) 99:3 *Vingtième Siècle. Revue d'Histoire*

Thirion, A. *Souvenirs Militaires* (Paris, 1892)

Tomes, N. 'The Quaker Connection: Visiting Patterns among Women in the Philadelphia Society of Friends, 1750–1800', in Zuckerman, M. (ed) *Friends and Neighbours: Group life in America's First Plural Society* (Temple, 1982) 186

Tone, JL. 'A Dangerous Amazon: Agustina Zaragoza and the Spanish Revolutionary War, 1808-1814' (2007) 37 *European History Quarterly* 4, 548-61

Var, L. (ed) *Campagnes du Capitaine Marcel du 69e de Ligne en Espagne et Portugal, 1808-1814* (Paris, 1914)

Vickery, A. *The Gentleman's Daughter* (Yale, 1998)

Vokins, J. *God's Mighty Power Magnified: As Manifested and Revealed in his Faithful Handmaid Joan Vokins* (1691)

Vourkoutiotis, V. *Prisoners of War and the German High Command. The British and American Experience* (Palgrave McMillan, 2003)

Wahrman, D. *The Making of the Modern Self: Identity And Culture in Eighteenth-Century England* (Yale, 2006)

Walker, TJ. *The Depot for Prisoners of War at Norman Cross, Huntingdonshire, 1796 to 1816* (Constable & Co., 1913)

Whittingham, F. (ed) *A Memoir of the Services of Samuel Ford Whittingham* (London, 1868)

Wolfe, R. *English Prisoners in France, containing Observations on their Manners and Habits* (Hatchard, 1830); *Register of Births, Marriages and Funerals of English Prisoners at Verdun, Givet and Elsewhere* (1803-1812)

Wollocombe, RH. *With the Guns in the Peninsula: the Peninsular-War Journal of Second Captain William Webber, Royal Artillery* (Greenhill, 1991)

Wright, S. 'Every Good Woman Needs a Companion of Her Own Sex: Quaker Women and Spiritual Friendship, 1750–1850', in Morgan, S. (ed) *Women, Religion and Feminism in Britain, 1750–1900* (Palgrave Macmillan, 2002); '"Truly Dear Hearts": Family and Spirituality in Quaker Women's Writings, 1680-1750', in Brown, S. (ed) *Women, Gender and Radical Religion in Early Modern Europe* (Brill, 2007)

Wulf, K. *Not all Wives: Women of Colonial Philadelphia* (Cornell, 2000)

Wylly, HC. (ed) *A Cavalry Officer in the Corunna Campaign: the Journal of Captain Gordon of the Fifteenth Hussars* (London, 1913)

Zanone, D. (ed) *Le Moi, l'Histoire: 1789-1848* (Ellug, 2005)

Lightning Source UK Ltd.
Milton Keynes UK
UKOW04f2315300315

248777UK00001B/1/P